Christmas Under Fire, 1944
The Last Christmas of World War II

Written by the same author:

War Zone Zoo
The Berlin Zoo and World War 2 (2018)
~~~

Christmas Under Fire, 1944

The Last Christmas of World War II

Kevin Prenger

Author: Kevin Prenger
www.kevinprenger.nl / Twitter @Kevin_Prenger
Translated by: Arnold van Wulfften Palthe
Cover designed by: Roger Paulussen
ISBN: 9781087410616
© 2019 Kevin Prenger

Cover: Illustration of Santa in army uniform (American Office for
Emergency Management War Production Board, 1942/1943): U.S.
National Archives
Photo author: Debbie van Dam

Index

Introduction

In 1944, Christmas was celebrated for the sixth time since the Second World War had broken out on September 1, 1939. Men who often shared the same religious background fought each other to the death in sharp contrast with the old Christmas message of Peace on Earth. What uniform a soldier wore at that moment or where he was made no difference, be it in a dormitory bunk on an R.A.F. base in England, aboard a destroyer in the Pacific, under the palm-leaf covered roof of a barracks in a Japanese POW camp, in a snowy foxhole on the Eastern front or at the controls of a bomber over Berlin. The yearning to be home for Christmas was universal among the armed forces of Christmas-celebrating countries during the war, especially in 1944. That Christmas, an Allied victory seemed within reach, which gave hope to many that the new year would finally bring peace.

During this last Christmas of the war, many military imagined they were at home but in reality, a peaceful Christmas with their families often seemed far away. If they were lucky, they would celebrate Christmas with their brothers in arms away from the firing line but many had to try and make something out of it, if at all possible, in the primitive situations at the front. In Bastogne, Budapest and other locations, fighting raged on uninterrupted during the Christmas holidays. To many POWs and civilians in captivity, their suffering did not end during those days. On the home front as well, bombardments, short-ages of food and other consequences of the war hampered the Christmas celebration in daily life.

Even in the most deplorable conditions during those frightful days, military, civilians, POWs and camp inmates alike celebrated Christmas. Food and drinks, presents, cheerful music, singing and other kinds of entertainment, gleaming decorations, religion, charity and being together with family and friends – all these ingredients of a Christmas celebration were there during the years of the war, albeit in adapted or limited form. In the war economy, luxury food, liquor, presents and Christmas decorations all disappeared from shops and tables during Christmas dinner. Family members who had been drafted into military service were absent. At the front and in the camps, privations during the Christmas celebrations were generally more severe although prisoners and POWs often displayed great powers of improvisation to make something festive out of the holidays. The human capability to celebrate Christmas even in the darkest of times and to draw hope from it is what this book is all about.

Minor subjects, like what was eaten during Christmas in times of rationing and shortages as well as major subjects such as important military and political events are reviewed. The emphasis is on Germany, Great Britain, the United States of America and the Netherlands, al-though some other Christmas-celebrating nations and nationalities will be covered as well.

This is no cheerful book, although it does contain cheerful and hopeful stories. First and foremost, this is a book about war. The memories of Christmas 1944 of many people were determined by bloody fighting, anxious hours in bomb shelters or terror in Nazi or Japanese camps. The absence of next of kin and the uncertainty about their fate were felt even more during the Christmas holidays. Homesickness, hunger and fear were felt more than joy. At the same time, celebrating Christmas included a promise of hope and peace. Peace that would enable a speedy reunion with family and friends.

These various experiences will be described in the chapters that follow. Quotations from memoirs, eyewitness accounts, interviews and letters will also be included. For a better understanding of the spirit of the times, newspaper articles and wartime news reels form an important source, but due to governmental censorship and propaganda these must be weighed critically, especially those of German origin. It is not the intention of this book to paint a general overview of Christmas in 1944. The major goal is to provide insight into how people of different nationalities and backgrounds experienced the last Christmas celebration of World War II and what kind of influence the big events of that time had on it.

- I -
Cold Turkey in the "Bulge"

After having set foot on French soil more than six months earlier, Allied troops in western Europe were looking forward to Christmas 1944. After the Normandy landings on June 6, part of western Europe had been liberated from the Nazi yoke. In the days prior to Christmas, preparations were made to give the soldiers a merry Christmas. After November 28, massive amounts of foodstuffs and drinks like Barclay's whisky and Guinness beer were unloaded at the port of Antwerp, liberated on September 4, to be distributed among the troops prior to the holidays.[1] Young, English-speaking Belgian women assisted in sorting the flow of Christmas mail for the troops. Small Christmas trees were harvested in the forests to be distributed among army hospitals.[2]

Paris and Brussels, liberated on August 25 and September 3 respectively, were designated official furlough cities and prepared themselves for the festivities. In the weeks before Christmas, soldiers with a valuable furlough pass had made many purchases in the restocked shops of the French capital. They bought luxury products for their girlfriends or wives back home such as perfume, lipstick and nylon stockings the average Parisian could impossibly afford. British military spent on average between 5 and 10 pounds, and due to their higher pay, their American colleagues would surely have exceeded this. In the shopping malls in Brussels, soldiers on leave bought Brussels lace, wine and cosmetics, but meat, tobacco, candy and clothing were still barely for sale, if at all. According to the British magazine *Picture Post*, "everything in Brussels costs the earth." A cup of coffee was 5 shillings and if one wanted to send a doll to one's daughter back home, it would easily set him back three weeks' pay.[3]

With the arrival of the Americans, bars and clubs in Brussels and Paris resounded with cheerful swing music to which Allied military danced the Jitterbug with attractive French or Belgian women who fell in droves for the sturdy charm of their liberators. Judy Garland's melancholic Christmas hit "Have yourself a Merry Little Christmas" could be heard blaring from the speakers as well, moving even battle-hardened warriors to tears. Probably the most popular song was Glenn Miller's "In the Mood". This swing tune by the American band leader had been released in the U.S. as early as 1939 but from 1944 on, it was freely distributed on record (V-Disc) to American military personnel overseas. Miller and his big band were expected in Paris for a Christmas performance for Allied troops.[4]

The cheerfulness among the Allies in Paris was mostly lost on the Parisians who were licking their wounds after an occupation of four years and who were not allowed to dance in their own cafés and dance halls. A few weeks earlier, the provisional government had banned it, arguing it would offend the many families mourning the deaths of loved ones and would be unfair toward the soldiers who were still imprisoned or fighting.[5]

Because fighting was still raging in Europe in December and the end of the war was not yet in sight, this cost Eisenhower 5 British pounds in a wager with Montgomery. On October 11, the American had put up stakes that Germany would be defeated before Christmas 1944. When he allowed Montgomery, more than a week before Christmas, to spend the holidays in England, the Allied commander-in-chief cheerfully indicated he had 9 days left to make his prediction come true. The U.S. Army Postal Service was just as optimistic and seriously took into account that the Christmas mail which had already arrived in Europe, would have to be returned the U.S.[6]

Yet, in December it was already clear that an Allied victory in 1944 was not achievable. The *Wehrmacht* kept up a vigorous defense, even after its losses in France and in Belgium. Operation Market Garden, the attempt by the Allies in September 1944 to establish a bridgehead between Arnhem and the IJsselmeer, had ended in failure, and the subsequent battle for the Hürtgen Forest had turned into a blood bath for the Americans, who counted 25,000 GIs killed in October and November alone.[7] It took an overwhelming force of American troops nearly three weeks to take Aachen, the first city on German soil to fall into Allied hands.[8] The Allied advance was delayed by shortages of fuel and ammunition and by overstretched supply lines. A massive offensive across the River Rhine was postponed until the new year, causing many soldiers on the Western Front to look forward to a Christmas celebration without the rattling of arms. They were to be deeply disappointed.

Despite losses on all fronts, Adolf Hitler still believed in a German victory in December 1944. The delay in the Allied advance provided him with an opportunity to launch a final, massive offensive, targeted at a sector of the Western Front, considered by the Allies to be quiet. The forests and rocky hills of the Ardennes were considered nearly impenetrable for German tanks and this 'ghost front' was mostly defended by exhausted American veterans of the Hürtgen Forest and by raw recruits, who had just arrived from the U.S. In some places, there was even some Christmas spirit, for instance in Arlon, which an American sergeant described as "untouched by war and the town and shops adorned with decorations and Christmas trees."[9] The assumption that the Germans would leave this sector of the front alone, was a miscalculation as it was right here that the *Wehrmacht* would attack along a front of 56 miles, deploying 13 infantry divisions, 2 armored brigades and 7 armored divisions, consisting of 250,000 men and 970 tanks, with the intention of advancing in the direction of the port of Antwerp and driving a wedge between American troops in the south and British and Canadian troops in the north.[10]

On December 11, the *Führer* arrived in his headquarters, the *Adlerhorst* (Eagle's Eyrie) north of Frankfurt from where he would closely follow Operation Wacht am Rhein (Guard on the Rhine).[11] When on the morning of December 16, after a short bombardment on the Allied lines, German tanks and troops appeared out of the fog, it came as a complete surprise to the Americans. The troops of the 1st Army, defending this sector under the command of General Courtney Hodges, could not prevent the Germans from penetrating up to 70 miles through the Allied lines before Christmas Eve. Owing to the bulge thus created in the Allied front, the battle for the Ardennes would become known as the Battle of the Bulge.

The Americans' plans for Christmas were abruptly aborted. Overwhelmed by the German attack, Major General Norman Cota, commanding the U.S. 28th Infantry Division in Wirth, Luxembourg, ordered all Christmas mail to be destroyed in order to prevent it from falling into German hands. A cloud of smoke rose from the inner court of his headquarters where letters, postcards and packages went up in flames.[12]

When the Allied lines in the Ardennes were breached by German troops, Corporal Gerald Nelson of the U.S. 7th Armored Division had just started decorating a Christmas tree in Verviers together with his mates. They had taken down the tree themselves and taken it to the building in which they were billeted. Celebrating Christmas with a roof over their heads – that was what Nelson and the other crews of the Sherman tanks were looking forward to when suddenly they received word they had to leave because of the German breakthrough at the front. They would have expected a transfer to the Pacific or even an earlier end of the war rather than a serious German attack. In the late afternoon of December 16, the unit left for Sankt-Vith, an important traffic junction that had to be defended against German capture. After having spent the night at the side of the road, the tank division made contact with the enemy the next day near Poteau. Nelson's tank commander was struck by a bullet as he fired the machine gun outside his turret. The corporal tried to bandage the wound in the back of his sergeant's head but failed to realize it had been completely blown away.[13]

Confused and afraid, many GIs fled from the German tanks and troops appearing before their eyes at various locations. In panic, they abandoned their equipment. All along the roads, which were filling up with German tanks and troops, stood American trucks, jeeps and other military vehicles which had been left behind during the chaotic retreat. Civilians with horses and carriages laden with their belongings also tried to escape to safer places over roads demolished by tanks.[14] Snow and cold made the exodus even more difficult. Due to the thick cloud cover, Allied aircraft were also grounded; so no air support could be provided during the first days. Rumors to the effect that German troops dressed in American uniforms had infiltrated in the Allied ranks – it did happen in some cases – and the execution of 84 American POWs by the SS near Malmédy only increased the fear and chaos.[15]

Nevertheless, both veterans and raw recruits managed to hold the Germans at bay in various locations. Although they were only a few miles away from the Meuse, their advance was behind schedule and fuel shortages threatened to endanger the operations. Meanwhile Eisenhower realized that the German attack was not just a pin prick, and on December 17, he dispatched both the U.S. 82nd and the 101st Airborne Divisions to the Ardennes. British forces were rushed in to protect the banks and crossing points of the Meuse River.[16]

The American paratroops had been looking forward to a different Christmas. In the vicinity of Reims, they were recuperating from their deployment in Operation Market Garden. After having been in the heat of the battle continuously, they hoped to go on leave and celebrate the holidays in Paris. For those of the 101st staying behind, a rugby match between the 506th PIR and 502nd PIR regiments was scheduled on Christmas Day, followed by a turkey dinner.[17] A trip to Paris or cheering for an exciting game followed by a good meal was now out of the question as they were loaded onto trucks and sent to the front along bumpy roads.

While the men of the 82nd were transferred to the northern flank, their colleagues of the 101st were sent to Bastogne, a centrally located city facing encirclement by German troops. From December 20 onwards, the siege of the city was a reality but then, the paratroops had already arrived to reinforce the local garrison. Just like the inhabitants of an invincible village in Gallia, the Americans put up a courageous resistance in order not to let the city, an important junction, slip out of their hands. They were short of almost everything – munitions, rations and medical supplies. Because of the weather, resupply from the air was out of the question. When the Germans, who were better equipped and superior in numbers, put an ultimatum to the Americans on December 22 to either surrender or be crushed, Brigadier General Anthony McAuliffe, deputy commander of the 101st Airborne, gave his legendary reply: "NUTS".[18]

The relief of besieged Bastogne would have to come not only from the air but also from the troops of Lieutenant General George Patton who were to relieve the city from the south but were being held up by the weather, German attacks and roads full of craters. The old fireeater, commander of U.S. 3rd Army, was itching to go from the beginning of December onwards, to advance from the north east of France towards the river Saar and the *Westwall,* but continuous rain held up his army. From his then headquarters in Nancy, he had phoned the Third Army's senior chaplain Colonel James O'Neill. "This is General Patton," he announced himself. "Do you have a good prayer for the weather? We have to do something about this rain if we want to win the war." The clergyman went ahead and composed a prayer of which 250,000 cards were printed and distributed among the troops from December 12 to 14.

The prayer reads in full: "Almighty and most merciful Father, we humbly beseech Thee, of Thy great goodness, to restrain these immoderate rains with which we have to contend. Grant us fair weather for Battle. Graciously hearken to us as soldiers who call Thee that, armed with Thy power, we may advance from victory to victory, and crush the oppression and wickedness of our enemies, and establish Thy justice among men and nations. Amen."

The card also contained a Christmas greeting from the general in which he expressed his confidence in the "courage, devotion to duty and skill in battle" of his men. "We march in our might to complete victory. May God's blessing rest upon each of you on this Christmas Day." To all 468 chaplains of the various religions within the 3rd Army as well as to all regimental commanders, an instruction was issued, urging them to pray together with their subordinates. The instruction included: "Those who pray do more for the world than those who fight; and if the world goes from bad to worse, it is because there are more battles than prayers."[19]

He proved that he was serious on December 23 when he, in spite of being Episcopalian himself, said a prayer in the Roman Catholic chapel of a home for the elderly in the city of Luxembourg. Here, he had established his headquarters which had been specially decorated for Christmas with German helmets with light bulbs.[20] The rain had turned to snow, still keeping Allied aircraft grounded; hence Patton's ground forces could not count on support from the air. Kneeling before the altar with a crucifix over his head, he tackled God on the fact that the past two weeks had been a real hell for his men: "rain, snow, more rain, more snow." He wondered: "Which side are You on? ... My army is neither trained nor equipped for war in winter. And as You know, this weather is more appropriate for Eskimos than for Southern riders." He ended his prayer by saying that "I do not even ask for a miracle, only four little days of beautiful weather."[21]

That very day the weather cleared and the Americans in besieged Bastogne were resupplied by Douglas C-47s escorted by P-47 Thunderbolts. The supplies dropped by parachute were received by cheering men on the ground. Over the following days, the Battered Bastards of Bastogne, as the paratroops of the 101st and other defenders of the town were called, received ample ammunition and rations to hold out longer.[22]

Despite the food drops, the Americans at the perimeter of the besieged town experienced a meager Christmas. On Christmas Eve, many found themselves in muddy fox holes or mortar emplacements in the snow-covered woods surrounding the town. Especially at night, it was bitterly cold. Those who did not regularly change their socks had to contend with trench foot or frostbite. Due to a lack of socks, strips of sheets were wrapped around feet. Men even froze to death in their sleep. While weapons and munition belts froze up and seized, condoms proved effective against frozen anti-tank gun visors. Men urinated on machine guns in order to thaw out the mechanism. At distant outposts, the supply of rations was bad, and men depended on the generosity of the locals or on whatever they could catch in nature. A hare shot by a sniper or a deer that had stepped onto a mine was a welcome addition to the frugal field rations. Meat from wild boars was better avoided as the animals fed on the corpses of dead soldiers.[23]

Protected by the twilight, some Americans left their safe fox holes on Christmas Eve for a moment in order to shake hands with their mates who had dug in next to them. They wished each other Merry Christmas and quickly returned to their own hiding places. At some locations the shouting of Christmas wishes sounded along entire American lines.[24] As far as is known, holiday greetings were not broadly conveyed to the enemy, as had sometimes been the case during World War I, but there are various reports of Americans who heard Germans singing Christmas carols behind enemy lines.[25]

Jack Womer of the 1st Demolition Section, 506th Parachute Infantry Regiment, 101st Airborne Division, participated in the defense of the perimeter around Bastogne. He recalled that he and his men had been under heavy German artillery fire for hours in the afternoon of the day before Christmas. "A lot of guys had been hit during the shelling despite the fact they'd been in their foxholes," Womer stated after the war. "Flying shrapnel usually found its way into a soldier's body even if he was taking cover. Sometimes artillery shells landed directly in a foxhole and exploded, and instantly killed anyone who was in it. A lot of guys were injured from trees that had been knocked down from exploding artillery. A tree would fall over a foxhole, and the limbs or large branches would drive into the foxhole and penetrate a man's body."

In the evening, the sound of exploding artillery shells was replaced by Christmas songs, played loudly by the Germans through their speakers in order to torment their opponents. Womer and his mates were located close enough to the German line to have to listen to this loud and clear annoyance. That Christmas Eve they were also showered with empty shells containing "Christmas cards" urging them to desert. Womer and his mates would not allow themselves to be trapped. Neither did they give up when later that night the artillery barrage was resumed until well after midnight.[26]

The Germans in the municipal prison in Bastogne were singing Christmas carols when General McAuliffe paid them a visit. As he wished them a Merry Christmas, his wish was answered by many voices wishing him the same.[27] That night, the general attended a few masses as well, such as with his men of the field artillery, somewhere on the outskirts of town.[28] In a letter distributed on Christmas Eve, McAuliffe wished his men a Merry Christmas. "What's Merry about all this, you ask," he began his message. "We're fighting – it's cold – we aren't home. All true but what has the proud Eagle Division accomplished with its worthy comrades of the 10th Armored Division, the 705th Tank Destroyer Battalion and all the rest? Just this: we have stopped cold everything that has been thrown at us from the North, East, South and West. ... How effectively this was done will be written in history; not alone in our Divison's glorious history but in world history. ... We are giving our country and our loved ones at home a worthy Christmas present and being privileged to take part in this gallant feat of arms are truly making for ourselves a Merry Christmas."[29] On Christmas Eve, the general also talked by phone to his superior, Major General Troy Middleton, saying that "the finest Christmas present the 101st could get would be a relief tomorrow."[30]

In Bastogne, conditions on Christmas Eve were in general only slightly better than at the front itself. Some 3,500 inhabitants who remained there tried to keep themselves warm and to protect themselves in basements and crypts of churches against German bombs and mortar shells.[31] A large number of them found shelter in the basement of the seminary for girls, Institut Notre Dame, that had been converted into a hospital by the Americans. During the day, so many wounded were brought in that some inhabitants had to make room for the patients. By the light of candles, the wounded were treated on their stretchers or on mattresses on the floor by medical orderlies assisted by civilians and nuns. A preacher encouraged them and performed the last rites for the dying. As the ground frequently reverberated from mortar bombs and shells exploding elsewhere in town, the girls of the boarding school impassively sang the Christmas carols they had picked up from the Americans. In the cellar, where a Christmas tree had been set up, the padre conducted a mass from behind a table which had been transformed into an altar. As the nuns were singing "Silent Night, Holy Night" in French, Americans joined them in English or Latin.[32]

Elsewhere on this cold Christmas Eve, soldiers found solace in religion as well. At the 101st Headquarters in a barracks in town, some 100 men attended a mass, conducted by a young chaplain in full garb. Christmas carols were sung accompanied by a small field organ. The priest called for confidence in God, as their fate now lay in His hands.[33]

However, Christmas Eve in Bastogne was not a quiet one. Using magnesium flares, German bombers, also taking advantage of the clear weather, dropped their bombs over the city causing widespread damage. It was the worst bombardment the city would have to endure during the war. Anti-aircraft weaponry to fight the bombers was not available as it was deployed on the outskirts of town.[34] In their stuffy subterranean shelters, at every explosion military and civilians feared being buried under the debris. Ambulances were racing through the streets to evacuate the wounded who had been rescued from beneath the rubble.

One of the bombs hit a medical aid station of the 20th Armored Infantry Battalion, which had been set up in a building near the railway station.[35] Over 100 injured lay in the cellar on sheets on the floor and were taken care of by two local Belgian nurses, Augusta Chiwy and Renée Lemaire, who had volunteered for duty. At the time of the bombardment, Augusta was in a nearby building where army surgeon Jack Prior had just uncorked his champagne bottle and filled the glasses of his colleagues. When the bomb struck, they were all thrown to the floor. As Prior, Chiwy and the others made their way out through clouds of dust, they feared the worst. Once outside they saw that the field hospital had collapsed and was on fire. The injured in the cellar were trapped beneath the burning remains of the building. Soldiers came running to extinguish the fire using buckets of water and to free the patients from the debris-covered cellar. Over 30 Americans could not be rescued and burned to death.[36]

The lifeless body of 30-year old nurse Lemaire was also recovered from the debris. Prior took her mutilated body, wrapped in a parachute, to her parents. She had been eager to use the same material for her wedding dress. In a letter to his commander, the army surgeon praised her services. "This girl cheerfully accepted the herculean task and worked without adequate rest or food until the night of her untimely death on 24 December 1944. ... Her very presence among those wounded men seemed to be an inspiration to those whose morale had declined from prolonged suffering. ... It is on these grounds that I recommend the highest award possible to one, who though not a member of the armed forces of the United States, was of invaluable assistance to us."[37]

The Angel of Bastogne, as the nurse would be called later, was posthumously awarded the U.S. Army Civilian Award for Humanitarian Service. The medal is on public display in the former headquarters of General McAuliffe in Bastogne, which is a museum today.[38] Augusta Chiwy was awarded the same decoration by the American Ambassador to Belgium on December 12, 2011. She passed away at the age of 94 on August 23, 2015, in the vicinity of Brussels.[39]

Fighting on Christmas Eve in Bastogne raged on inexorably. In various locations, German attacks were repulsed. "Xmas Eve present is coming. Hold on," Patton had radioed that morning to McAuliffe, meaning the relief of Bastogne by his tanks.[40] In the besieged city, they would have to wait for that until after Christmas. On Christmas Eve in the Anglican church in Luxembourg, Patton attended mass by candlelight, sitting on the church bench of the last German emperor.[41] That same day, he had awarded his chaplain, Colonel O'Neill, with the Bronze Star medal for the alleged influence his prayer had had on the weather. "Chaplain, you must be the most popular man in this Headquarters. You sure stand in good with the Lord and soldiers," as Patton complimented him.[42]

On Christmas morning, the general noted in his diary: "A clear, cold Christmas, lovely weather for killing Germans, which seems a bit queer, seeing whose birthday it is."[43] He was to have his Christmas dinner in the Alfa Hotel where his staff had decorated a Christmas tree with fragments of the windscreen of a downed bomber, but first he inspected his troops in the field who had been promised a turkey dinner.

The American journalist William Strand reported from the front in Belgium that turkey would be served at the front as well as in the areas behind the front. For every 100 men, 100 pounds of meat was available "with everything that usually goes with it." He did add however that this could only be done "if there is time, that is; otherwise, the dinner will be kept in fireless cookers until the doughboys have a respite from fighting to enable them to line up and have it piled – tiny square mince pie and all – into their mess kits, where it will look like anything but an American Christmas dinner."[44] Often, the turkey was already cold before it was served to the troops.

Brigadier General Anthony McAuliffe and his staff during Christmas dinner on December 25, 1944. (U.S. Army / U.S. National Archives)

In Bastogne, most military had to make do without turkey. For instance, the men of Easy Company, 506th PIR, had cold white beans and cold broth. In his headquarters, McAuliffe and his staff officers enjoyed tinned salmon, biscuits and lemon meringue pie made of donut flour and K-ration lemonade. They ate at a neatly laid table with a cheery centerpiece of decorated fir branches topped by a paper star.[45]

Americans who had been made POWs during the Ardennes offensive often missed a Christmas dinner. This did not apply to Private Joe Tatman of the 9th Armored Division who, along with a few others, was hiding behind the German lines in a hay stack outside Bastogne on December 24. Their food supply was running out and they encouraged themselves with tales of Christmas at home. Around 16:00 hours they were discovered by the Germans and forced to surrender. The Americans would have been surprised when they were addressed in their own language by a German captain. The officer was a lawyer in New York, but he had been drafted into the *Wehrmacht* after he had traveled to his fatherland in order to see to the inheritance of his father. He took his prisoners to a nearby farm house where he gave them milk and something to eat.

While the Americans enjoyed the treats, the German talked with them about the war and cracked jokes about it. He hoped the war would soon be over enabling everyone to return home. Next he gave them hot water, towels and shaving kits so they could refresh themselves as the occupants of the farm – an elderly Belgian couple – had invited them to a Christmas dinner. They sat down at a beautifully laid table and were served all sorts of food, including meat. There even were American cigarettes. When dinner was done, they sang "Silent Night" – the prisoners in English and their guards in German. At the end, the German captain proposed a toast to the Americans. He explained he had granted them this moment of relaxation as on the following morning, Christmas Day, they would begin their "journey to hell", meaning their transfer to a prisoner-of-war camp.[46] The conditions during these voyages were often miserable: miles and miles of marching without food, drink or sleep were usually followed by train rides in cattle cars which were frequently interrupted by bombings.

An even more remarkable event of rare fraternization between enemies took place on Christmas Eve during the Ardennes offensive in a hunting lodge in the Hürtgen Forest. Three German and three American soldiers enjoyed a mutual Christmas dinner while nearby the Ardennes offensive raged on in full intensity. In the winter of 1944-1945, the lodge was inhabited by Elisabeth Vincken and her 12-year old son Fritz. The head of the family, a professional baker was serving in the *Reichsluftschützdienst* (air raid protection service) in the German city of Monschau, a few miles away. As their resident town of Aachen was targeted by Allied bombardments, mother and son had found a safe haven in the lodge Herr Vincken used for his hunting trips. Fritz and his mother had hoped his dad would celebrate Christmas Eve with them, but when he did not show up, they decided to postpone their Christmas dinner until New Year's Day.

A knock on the door heralded the beginning of an evening that took a quite unexpected turn. When Elisabeth opened the door, she stood face to face with three American soldiers of whom one was seriously injured. They meant no harm and were only looking for a warm shelter to recuperate after they had gotten lost and had been wandering in the cold for three days, looking for their battalion. The Americans did not speak German but one of them was able to communicate with the woman in French. She invited the young men in who could well have been her sons. The injured American was carried inside by his comrades and put down on the bed of the boy.

The GIs introduced themselves as Jim, Robin and Harry. The hostess decided to serve the postponed Christmas dinner to her famished guests. The fattened rooster she had called Hermann (after *Reichsmarschall* Hermann Göring) was put into the oven, and Fritz started laying the table for five. As Jim assisted in the cooking, Robin saw to his injured mate Harry. He had a bullet wound in his upper leg, and this was bandaged by the woman with strips torn off a sheet. As the hut in the forest filled with the delicious smell from the oven, there was another knock on the door. Fritz expected more lost Americans but as he opened the door he froze with fear seeing three German soldiers. Giving shelter to Allied soldiers was punishable by death, he knew. Elisabeth rushed to the door and welcomed the *Wehrmacht* soldiers by wishing them a Merry Christmas. The men, very young like the Americans, told her they had lost their regiment and asked permission to stay in the lodge for the night. The woman approved and offered the men a hot meal which the hungry soldiers naturally did not reject. "But we have three other guests whom you may not consider friends," Elisabeth continued. "This is Christmas Eve and there will be no shooting here," she warned them in a firm voice. The Germans, two soldiers and a corporal, understood the woman was hiding Americans but decided to obey her. The left their weapons on a stack of fire wood and entered the warm lodge. On her request, the Americans also handed over their weapons to the woman. Inside the lodge, no one had counted on so many guests so two Germans and two Americans sat down on the bed of their hostess.

Initially the atmosphere was rather tense, but gradually the tension lifted. One of the Germans spoke English and, being a medical student, he was able to assess the physical condition of the injured soldier. He concluded the man had lost much blood but owing to the cold, the wound was not infected. Rest and good care would make him feel much better. Put at ease over their mutual good intentions, the soldiers did justice to the fattened rooster. The Germans shared a loaf of bread and a bottle of red wine with the Americans. Half of the wine was kept by the woman for the injured soldier.

The truce in the lodge lasted until the following morning. The men were given a plate of oatmeal porridge, and she made a restorative drink of egg, sugar and the rest of the wine for the American with the leg wound. In order to transport him, a stretcher was constructed from wooden poles and a table cloth. Thereafter, the Americans and Germans went their separate ways but not before the German corporal had shown his enemies the right direction to the American lines first and also gave them a compass. Prior to the soldiers' departure, Elisabeth returned their weapons to them. "Be careful boys," she said. "I want you to get home someday where you belong." The Germans and the Americans shook hands and disappeared in opposite directions.[47]

Over 40 years later, on May 5, 1985, the story mentioned above was recalled to memory by Ronald Reagan. The Cold War was still raging and the American president had traveled to Germany to celebrate 40 years of peace between Germany and the United States. Shortly before making a speech at the American air base in the city of Bitburg, he had laid a wreath in the local German war cemetery. Reagan's visit to the war cemetery had initially evoked a lot of commotion. In particular because of the presence of graves of soldiers from the hated *Waffen-SS*, many American veterans and survivors of the Holocaust considered it inappropriate that their president attended the memorial service. In his speech, Reagan stated: "I felt great sadness that history could be filled with such waste, destruction and evil. But my heart was also lifted by the knowledge that from the ashes has come hope, and that from the terrors of the past we have built 40 years of peace and freedom –and reconciliation among our nations." He was sorry his visit was so controversial and he assured American veterans and their next of kin that "our gesture of reconciliation with the German people today in no way minimizes our love and honor for those who fought and died for our country." He promised the survivors of the Holocaust that reconciliation did not mean forgetting. In the morning he had been in the former Bergen-Belsen concentration camp where he became even more strongly convinced of the credo "never again."

During his speech, the American president said that out of the more than 2,000 soldiers buried in the Bitburg cemetery, only 48 had served in the *Waffen-SS*. He indicated he did not believe in collective guilt. In his opinion, many victims had been just normal, often young soldiers. "How many were fanatic followers of a dictator and willfully carried out his cruel orders?" he asked his audience. "And how many were conscripts, forced into service during the death throes of the Nazi war machine?" He said that one of the soldiers in the cemetery was killed a week before his 16th birthday. In the cemetery he honored the German war victims as "human beings, crushed by a vicious ideology."

Halfway through his speech, Reagan touched upon the story about the Christmas Eve in the hunting lodge of the German Vincken family during the Ardennes offensive. His staff had found the story written by Fritz Vincken in the *Reader's Digest* edition of January 1973, entitled "Truce in the Forest." The story seemed to be custom-made to be used in the President's speech as a symbol of the brotherhood between two nations in which, in his words, "the hope we see now could sometimes even be glimpsed in the darkest days of the war."[48] That the six soldiers in the lodge in the Hürtgenwald had also been very young closely linked to his earlier argument.

Listening to the radio during a break, Fritz Vincken was surprised to hear the American president recite his story. The German had left the country in 1959, and after having lived in Canada and California he had settled down in Hawaii in 1963. In the Kapalama suburb of Honolulu he opened Fritz' European Bakery, where the sales girls were dressed in dirndls (traditional southern German and Austrian dress). The residents of the island were standing in line for the German brown bread and the *Schwarzwalder Kirschtorte* (a delicacy from the Black Forest).[49] Fritz was a staunch admirer of Ronald Reagan and was touched by his words. Urged by American friends, he had written down his memories of Christmas Eve 1944 and had sent them to *Readers' Digest*. His story of the Christmas evening in the hunting lodge seems too good to be true, but it probably did take place. Prior to Reagan's speech in Germany, the White House staff had the authenticity of the story checked by *Reader's Digest*. The editors of the magazine indicated that prior to publication, an experienced research journalist had conducted a thorough investigation. Elisabeth Vincken had been traced in Aachen and she had told the exact same story as her son, without having read the text before. Local research had been conducted as well, for instance by speaking to local inhabitants. "We're convinced, without a doubt, that the story is true," the confident former editor in chief stated.[50] In 1995, one of the soldiers in the story was tracked down by the producers of an American television program.[51]

Whether or not men were being served turkey – or fried rooster in a hunting lodge – in some cases they were creative enough to scrape together something tasty on their own. John Otto was a lieutenant in the 82nd Airborne and wanted to do something special at Christmas for the men under his command. They were short of shoes and clothing, and after Operation Market Garden they were actually far from ready to be deployed at the front again. Otto himself had just been discharged from hospital where he had been nursed after having been shot down over the Netherlands. In the Ardennes, a medic from his unit risked his life every day in order to milk a goat in a barn close to the house in which they were billeted. Each time on the way out and back, the man was shot at by the Germans but he was never hit.

The radio operator of the unit, a baker in peace time, managed to find some flour, and another boy found some apples. Otto himself collected sugar by taking it from the rations of his men. They were not happy to have to make do without sugar for a while, but the lieutenant blamed company HQ. With those ingredients, the baker made apple pie which was distributed among the men on the front line. "It was their Christmas present," Lieutenant Otto declared after the war. "It worked real nice. I told them, 'Here's the damned sugar you were bitching about.'"[52]

On the Ardennes front as well, Christmas without booze was not complete for many men. A captain of the 22nd Regiment, 4th Infantry Division, had been given a half bottle of Scotch by a fellow officer. Instead of drinking it himself or sharing it with fellow officers, he selected seven of his men who had repulsed German attacks for nine days on end at the front. They all handed over their powdered orange juice from their rations, mixing it with the scotch and water from their flasks. Subsequently they heated this concoction over a pile of burning ration boxes. On Christmas Eve, at midnight, the brew was served. "Next morning," a veteran remembers, "an E company lieutenant and one of his men crept through the woods to the nearest enemy position, killed the two Germans in it, took a light machine-gun and made their way safely back to the command post, and presented the weapon to their commander – the same officer who had shared the scotch with his men – as a gift. Merry Christmas ... but not for those German boys."[53]

The Christmas of infantryman Raymond Gantter was far from festive. The main reason was a physical disorder, known among soldiers as "the GIs". From an undisclosed location on the Belgian-German border, Gantter wrote a letter to his parents on December 25, wishing them a Merry Christmas. On Christmas Eve, he and his mates had relieved a unit that had spent a few days in the front line. "So I spent Christmas Eve and will spend Christmas Day in a dugout facing the German lines. Ah there, Adolf! *Fröhliche Weihnachten!*" During the "beautiful and grim Christmas Eve" he changed the guard with his mate Shorty. "The cold I could endure, but an additional misery landed on me in the middle of the night. I got the GIs! That's always a tragedy, of course – although in normal life, with the luxury of a civilized bathroom at hand, it would seem only an embarrassing annoyance – but this time the tragedy was of major proportions." He lay dug in on the crest of a hill with no shrubs or trees anywhere near to seek cover. "It's not modesty that bothers us, you understand: it's snipers," he explained. Each time he felt the need, he looked fearfully in the direction of the German lines, unbuttoned his trousers and climbed out of his shelter, holding up his trousers with one hand and subsequently hastily relieved himself, hoping not to be noticed by a German sniper.

"A half-naked man crouching on a hilltop is a defenseless creature," Gantter wrote his parents, "unnerved by the constant sense of his nakedness framed in the sights of an enemy rifle. I winced and shook each time I dropped my pants, expecting every moment to be caponized by a German sniper who combined marksmanship with a macabre sense of humor." The unlucky American fortunately remained unnoticed by the enemy. He remembered the artillery barrage continuing until midnight after which it petered out. "In the strange silence, the war seemed remote, and I was several thousand miles from Belgium for a few moments."

He and his mate got no breakfast that Christmas morning. Their squad leader forgot to send a messenger to tell them to come to eat. Gantter wrote: "We waited and hoped and peered anxiously for sight of the runner until there was no longer any point in hoping. Except that it was Christmas morning, I did not mind the missed meal: my interior was worn out after my late tussle with the GIs." Breakfast for the two Americans did not consist of much more than a little coffee and a tin of C-rations they shared among them. Shorty ate a can of cold hash (a mix of cooked chopped meat and cooked chopped potatoes) as well. Gantter recalls: "We munched in unhappy silence and I brooded over the memory of our customary Christmas stollen (how ironically German), so richly stuffed with raisins and nuts and citron."[54]

Some place farther down the line, Russell Albrecht experienced an even worse Christmas. He was in the northern sector of the battlefield and suffered from a major pain in the chest. "I couldn't even stand a teaspoon in my breast pocket," he wrote in his memoirs, "it felt like it was too heavy against my chest." He was given permission to leave his position in order to get some aspirin in Malmédy, about a mile away, where a few physicians stayed. Although the distance was not very long, it still was an arduous trip as it had to be made on hands and knees to avoid being shot at, the question being what he had to fear most, enemy or friendly fire.

On Christmas Day, the sick American decided to go to the town. "I just kind of lay flat in the snow and sneaked along, staying behind whatever I could. I got in there and saw some smoke coming out of a house, and I went over there. There were some tank soldiers inside who were warming themselves behind closed shutters." They gave their guest some water with which he made a cup of instant coffee. He also used the short break to write a letter to his wife and daughters. After he had learned that some doctors had moved into a house some distance away, he went to see them. The doctors were just eating turkey but one of them interrupted his Christmas dinner to take the patient's temperature. "He went back in to chew down some more turkey, and then he came back in and looked and kind of frowned – he got some more equipment, started testing and pretty soon told the guys, 'You get a stretcher for this guy.'" Russell was put on a stretcher and a label was attached to his jacket with the ominous diagnosis: "Bronchitis, Pleurisy and Pneumonia." Thanks to his daring trip to Malmédy and the attention of a doctor he survived, in contrast to his mate with whom he had shared a shelter: he reportedly was killed by a direct hit the next day.[55]

The Americans transferred many seriously injured from the Ardennes offensive to the city of Luxembourg where the 104th Evacuation Hospital, a unit of Patton's 3rd Army, had established itself in a home for the elderly and orphans. Nurse May Albertine Buelow, 28 years old and a Canadian national, was a member of the medical staff – a 1st Lieutenant in the U.S. Army Nurse Corps. She had spent a few months in Liverpool; then she had landed on Omaha Beach, 35 days after D-Day. During the passage across the English Channel in an LCI (Landing Craft Infantry), she and the other nurses had been obliged to wear long Johns under their dresses. She arrived in Luxembourg in the afternoon of December 24 with a column of ambulances driven by nurses via Paris and Nice. They hardly had time to set up their medical aid post because that same night the first injured arrived and the hospital became fully operational. "We were extremely busy caring for the wounded" arriving in "ambulances and [on] litters strapped to jeeps to carry the wounded. The receiving area, triage, was soon inundated and surgery became a very busy place." Stomach injuries, facial wounds and amputations had priority. Along with "three wonderful corpsmen" they kept the boilers in operation in which surgical equipment was being sterilized. At night, they ate their C-rations by the light of flash lights as the kitchens had not yet been set up and a regular meal could not be made.

According to the nurse, Christmas Day in Luxembourg was "cloudy and bitter cold. The ground was frozen and covered with snow. There was a feeling of foreboding. I was in the middle of a war!" By day, she and her colleagues were busy in their work and there was no time to celebrate Christmas. Instead of turkey, they again ate their C-rations. After a few days, the work lessened a little and the cooks managed to serve a turkey dinner.

On Christmas Day itself, Nurse Buelow and her colleagues distributed presents among at least 40 of the orphans who, unlike the elderly, were still in the building. The children were surprised with sweets and other small items from the Christmas boxes the nurses had received in Nancy. In the evening, off-duty staff members including Nurse Buelow attended a religious service in town where Patton's Christmas message was read.[56] In a letter to her grandparents, aunt and other next of kin, dated December 31st, she wrote that things had finally quieted down a little as other hospitals had been opened. It was snowing and during a stroll through the old town, which she enjoyed very much, she saw children sledding down the hills. She let it be known however that "there's a lot of war to be fought yet. Things appear more encouraging for us again but the price is terrific. One only needs to see one casualty to realize that."[57] As late as November 1945, the nurse would return to the U.S. after having been active in five campaigns in two years. Prior to her honorable discharge, she was promoted to Captain.[58]

On the German side of the front during the Ardennes offensive, Christmas celebrations were hardly different. In the towns and villages where they had chased the Americans out, many German soldiers celebrated Christmas in the homes in which they were billeted. They often took possession of the finest rooms and had the women and girls do the cooking and perform other household chores.[59] The Belgians and Luxembourgers were usually not happy with their return after they had been liberated by the Allies a few months earlier.

However, the Germans who returned did not necessarily behave themselves like the cruel oppressor towards the civilians.

Quite often, civilians and German military celebrated Christmas together. The German infantryman, Gottfried Kischkel, and his mates, for instance, shared with the Belgian family on Christmas Eve two tins of ham they had found in the house where they were billeted. Together they sat at a large circular table and had, in addition to the ham, bread, potatoes and a fruit salad for dinner. They all drank apple cider from the family stock. During dinner the head of the household rose and introduced himself as the mayor of the village. "Although our countries are at war," he declared, "I came from German ancestry, as you can hear from my accent. This feast is a friendly gesture to you, as you are all poor young men so unlucky to find yourself fighting a war on Christmas Day."[60]

Elsewhere, the Germans also shared their rations with civilians, even if they hadn't much to share themselves. *Oberst* Heinz Kokott, commander of the *26. Volksgrenadier-Division* in Bras, a mere 18.5 miles west of Bastogne, shared chocolate and cookies with children and wished them a Merry Christmas. Of course, the German did not tell them that all those goodies had come from supplies dropped by the Americans.[61]

Josef Schröder, a fellow country man of commander Kokott and a member of the *15. Fallschirm-Jäger-Regiment*, helped a mother in distress in Bigonville, Luxembourg although not entirely of his own free will. In the morning of December 24, the village in which he and a few others had hidden in a cellar in order to escape to German lines when darkness fell, was surrounded by the American 26th Infantry Division. As the Americans attacked in the afternoon, he left his hiding place after two grenades had been thrown inside causing injury to no one. He was forced to surrender as his ammunition had run out. The German was taken away by two American soldiers and was made to stand with his face against the wall. It looked grim for him until an officer intervened and saved him from possible execution. The Americans took him to a woman who had taken refuge in a cellar with her new-born baby. She needed help for her baby who was crying, but she spoke no English; so the officer needed Schröder as an interpreter. In broken English the German managed to make clear to the Americans that the baby needed milk but that the mother could not feed it. Thereupon a cow was found which was immediately milked by the German after which they both returned to the hungry baby. "When we stood around that child or were on our knees,"

Schröder recalled afterwards, "and gave the mother a small bottle of milk for the child, I did not have the feeling an enemy was standing next to me. It was somebody who cared about a human life just as much as I did."[62] Thanks to the temporary cooperation between two enemies, mother and child survived the war.

In various locations, Germans and civilians attended masses together. After a local priest had celebrated mass in a cellar in Sibret, some 6.5 miles southeast of Bastogne, a German chaplain took over while the attending civilians made room for soldiers. At the end, both priests hugged each other.[63] In Remoiville, some 6.5 miles south of Sibret, locals and Germans shared the space in a cellar. People recited the Ave Maria until a German soldier started humming "Silent Night." He was listened to breathlessly until a comrade ordered the singer to stop singing. It probably had become too much for him.[64]

When a school teacher returned after Christmas to his ruined class room in Champs, some 5 miles southeast of Bastogne, he read a special message on the blackboard, written by a German officer: "May the world never again live through such a Christmas night. Nothing is more horrible than meeting one's fate, far from mother, wife and children. ... Life was bequeathed us in order that we might love and be considerate to one another. From this ruins, out of blood and death, shall come forth a brotherly world."[65]

In spite of the reflection of the German officer on the black board and all examples of fraternization between Germans and civilians, many inhabitants in the Ardennes experienced Christmas as a hell at the hands of others from the same Germany. An horrendous event took place on Christmas Eve in Bande where 32 males between the ages of 17 and 32 were executed by the German *Sicherheitsdienst* (SD), looking for resistance fighters who were responsible for the death of Belgian collaborators. Their corpses were dumped in the basement of a burnt-out house. On Christmas Day, two more young men were murdered at the same location by the Germans. Boards were thrown over the corpses and gradually covered in snow. It was not before the new year, on January 11, that British military discovered the remains based on directions by Abbot Jean Baptiste, who had three pupils among the victims.[66]

Numerous other innocent civilians were unintentionally injured or killed by the violence of war that raged in their home towns. During American bombardments on St. Vith and Malmédy during the Christmas period, nearly 400 civilians were killed.[67] Also in Malmédy, 37 American soldiers of the 30th Infantry Division died in a bombardment by their own air force, which they angrily called the American *Luftwaffe*.[68] Hundreds of inhabitants of Malmédy were hiding in caves in the north of the city during the Christmas holidays while a large part of their city was bombed to rubble by their liberators, who did not realize they were dropping their bombs on a city that had been in Allied hands since September 11, 1944.[69] Children in Malmédy had previously been given Red Cross parcels by those friendly American soldiers.[70]

After having repulsed ferocious German attacks again on Christmas Day, towards 17:00 hours on December 26, the Christmas present promised to the beleaguered troops in Bastogne finally arrived. Tanks of the 4th Armored Division trundled into the city, lifting the siege that had lasted seven days. "Cobra King", the tank of 1st Lieutenant Charles P. Boggess of the 37th Tank Battalion, was the first to arrive. "First in Bastogne" the proud crew wrote on the armor of their vehicle.[71] The greatest feat had been achieved by the 101st Airborne Division and the other units that fought there, without which the city would surely have been captured by the Germans. The division was awarded a Presidential Unit Citation for their "extraordinary heroism and gallantry in defense of this key communication center in Bastogne."[72] It was the first time that this honor fell to an entire division. The unit had paid a high price though: the 101st lost 1,536 men and 105 officers; the 10th Armored Division lost 478 men and 25 officers.[73]

The relief of Bastogne did not put an end to the Ardennes offensive though. The battle raged on until January 25 after all German units had been pushed back towards the *Westwall*. The *Wehrmacht* had failed to cross the river Meuse but the consequences of Hitler's "last gamble" were bloody. Military historian Antony Beevor calls the Ardennes offensive "the largest and most barbaric battle of the entire western front."[74] The Americans mourned a total of 80,987 casualties, including 10,276 deaths and over 23,218 missing; the British had 1,408 casualties including 200 dead, the Germans had 98,024 casualties, including 12,000 dead and over 30,000 missing. Some 3,000 civilians lost their lives as well.[75]

Notes chapter I:

[1] Christmas Ration for Troops (1944), British Pathé.
[2] 'Allied Services Christmas Celebration Greetings', British Pathé.
[3] Brown, M., *Christmas on the Home Front*, p. 179.
[4] *Kerst aan het front*, EO Tweede Wereldoorlog documentaires, 2005.
[5] Cooper, A. & Beevor, A., *Paris After the Liberation: 1944 – 1949*, p. 91.
[6] Weintraub, S., *11 in December*, pp. 2, 9.
[7] Weintraub, S., *11 Days in December*, p. 22.
[8] Thompson, J., *De bevrijding*, p. 24.
[9] Ambrose, S.E., *Citizen Soldiers*, p. 254.
[10] Toland, J., *Battle: The Story of the Bulge*, p. 26; Thompson, J., *De bevrijding*, p. 28.
[11] Short, N., *The Führer's Headquarters: Hitler's command bunkers 1939–45*, p. 41.
[12] Weintraub, S., *11 Days in December*, p. 40.
[13] Weintraub, S., *11 Days in December*, p. 32.
[14] Hull, M.D., 'Christmas in Embattled Bastogne', *Warfare History Network*, 1 Mai 2017.
[15] Beevor, A., *Het Ardennenoffensief*, pp. 90, 133.
[16] Hull, M.D., 'Christmas in Embattled Bastogne', *Warfare History Network*, 1 Mai 2017.
[17] Weintraub, S., *11 Days in December*, p. 43.
[18] 'McAuliffe's Kerstboodschap aan de 101st Division (24 Dec. 1944)', Traces-OfWar.nl.
[19] O'Neill, J.H., 'The True Story of the Patton Prayer', *The New American*, 12 Jan. 2004.
[20] 20 Beevor, A., 'The Christmas Day the snow turned red', *The Daily Mail*, 24 Dec. 2015.
[21] Baraitre, I., *Patton: Een Generaal in de Ardennen*, pp. 227-228.
[22] Schrijvers, P., *Those Who Hold Bastogne*, p. 100.
[23] Beevor, A., 'The Christmas Day the snow turned red', *The Daily Mail*, 24 Dec. 2015.
[24] Hull, M.D., 'Christmas in Embattled Bastogne', *Warfare History Network*, 1 Mai 2017.
[25] The Library of Congress, *I'll Be home for Christmas*, p. 121.
[26] Womer, J. & DeVito, S.C., *Fighting with the Filthy Thirteen*, pp. 233-242.
[27] Corsi, J., *No Greater Valor: The Siege of Bastogne and the Miracle That Sealed Allied Victory*, pp. 249-250.
[28] Hull, M.D., 'Christmas in Embattled Bastogne', *Warfare History Network*, 1 Mai 2017.
[29] 'Gen. Anthony McAuliffe's Christmas Message to his troops', 24 Dec. 1944, on: www.archivesfoundation.org/documents/surrender-nuts-gen-anthony-mcauliffes-1944-christmas-message-troops/.

[30] Corsi, J., *No Greater Valor: The Siege of Bastogne and the Miracle That Sealed Allied Victory*, p. 256.

[31] Hull, M.D., 'Christmas in Embattled Bastogne', *Warfare History Network*, 1 Mai 2017.

[32] Schrijvers, P., *The Unknown Dead: Civilians in the Battle of the Bulge*, pp. 211-212.

[33] Weintraub, S., *11 Days in December*, p. 137.

[34] Beevor, A., 'The Christmas Day the snow turned red', *The Daily Mail*, 24 Dec. 2015.

[35] Hull, M.D., 'Christmas in Embattled Bastogne', *Warfare History Network*, 1 Mai 2017.

[36] Beevor, A., 'The Christmas Day the snow turned red', *The Daily Mail*, 24 Dec. 2015; Hull, M.D., 'Christmas in Embattled Bastogne', *Warfare History Network*, 01 Mai 2017.

[37] Prior, J.T., 'The Night Before Christmas – Bastogne, 1944', *The Onondaga County Medical Society Bulletin*, Dec. 1972.

[38] Exposition Bastogne Barracks.

[39] Roberts, S., 'Augusta Chiwy, 'Forgotten' Wartime Nurse, Dies at 94', *The New York Times*, 25 Aug. 2015.

[40] Weintraub, S., *11 Days in December*, p. 109.

[41] Beevor, A., 'The Christmas Day the snow turned red', *The Daily Mail*, 24 Dec. 2015.

[42] Weintraub, S., *11 Days in December*, p. 132; Patton, G.S., *War As I Knew It*, p. 186.

[43] Weintraub, S., *11 Days in December*, p. 152.

[44] Strand, W., 'In Belgian Front Line', *Chicago Tribune*, 25 Dec. 1944.

[45] Barron, L. & Cygan, D., *No Silent Night: The Christmas Battle For Bastogne*, p.285; Weintraub, S., *11 Days in December*, p. 164.

[46] Ambrose, S.E., *Citizen Soldiers*, p. 270.

[47] Vincken, F. 'Truce in the Forest', *Reader's Digest*, Jan. 1973, pp. 111-114.

[48] 'Remarks at a Joint German-American Military Ceremony at Bitburg Air Base in the Federal Republic of Germany', 5 Mai 1985, The Ronald Reagan Presidential Library and Museum.

[49] Ohira, R., 'Fritz Vincken, bakery owner, dead at 69', *Honolulu Advertiser*, 11 Jan. 2002.

[50] Saxon, W., 'President Cites a Story of Peace amid the Terrors of Battle', The New York Times, 6 Mai 1985.

[51] Ohira, R., 'Fritz Vincken, bakery owner, dead at 69', *Honolulu Advertiser*, 11 Jan. 2002.

[52] Burger, T.W., 'Christmas under the Gun', *America in WWII*, Dec. 2005.

[53] 225th AAA Searchlight Battalion Veterans Association, Skylighters.org.

[54] Gantter, R., *Roll Me Over: An Infantryman's World War II*, p. 99.

[55] Berger, F., *Finding Foxholes*.

56 Alm, M.A., 'Christmas 1944 - Battle of the Bulge: A Christmas That Wasn't Christmas', www.crystalsw.com, 22 Nov. 1998.

57 Alm, M.A., 'Letter from Luxembourg', 31 Dec. 1944.

58 Alm, M.A., 'Christmas 1944 - Battle of the Bulge: A Christmas That Wasn't Christmas', www.crystalsw.com, 22 Nov. 1998.

59 Schrijvers, P., *The Unknown Dead: Civilians in the Battle of the Bulge*, p. 134.

60 Ambrose, S.E., *Citizen Soldiers*, p. 247.

61 Schrijvers, P., *The Unknown Dead: Civilians in the Battle of the Bulge*, p. 204; Weintraub, S., *11 Days in December*, p. 150.

62 *Kerst aan het front*, EO Tweede Wereldoorlog documentaires, 2005; Schröder, J., 'Milk: A Christmas Story', www.bigonville.info.

63 Schrijvers, P., *The Unknown Dead: Civilians in the Battle of the Bulge*, p. 204.

64 Schrijvers, P., *The Unknown Dead: Civilians in the Battle of the Bulge*, p. 205.

65 The Library of Congress, *I'll be Home for Christmas*, p. 121.

66 Weintraub, S., *11 Days in December*, pp. 116-117; Schrijvers, P., *The Unknown Dead: Civilians in the Battle of the Bulge*, p. 251.

67 Tourist Info St. Vith, www.st.vith.be; Le Royal Syndicat d'Initiative de Malmedy, www.malmedy.be.

68 Delaforce, P., *The Battle of the Bulge: Hitler's Final Gamble*, p. 205.

69 'Liberation memorial Malmedy' + 'Shelter Civilians Malmedy', TracesofWar.com.

70 Weintraub, S., *11 Days in December*, pp. 139-140.

71 Melancon, D., "Cobra King' led 4th Armored Division column that relieved Bastogne during Battle of the Bulge', *Army Europe Public Affairs Office*, 25 Feb. 2009.

72 Presidential Unit Citation for Bastogne 101st Airborne Division and Attached Units, Mourmelon, France, 15 Mar. 1945.

73 Corsi, J., *No Greater Valor: The Siege of Bastogne and the Miracle That Sealed Allied Victory*, p. 285.

74 Beevor, A., 'The Christmas Day the snow turned red', *The Daily Mail*, 24 Dec. 2015.

75 Weintraub, S., *11 Days in December*, pp. 177-178.

- II -
A Merry Little Christmas

Slippers and king size cigarettes were the Christmas gifts, Mamie Eisenhower had sent to her husband in Versailles.[1] In the city that breathed the atmosphere of the former French Empire and where the armistice ending the First World War had been signed between Germany and the Allied nations, the commander-in-chief had established his headquarters in the Hotel Trianon Palace, an elegant building on the edge of the park that belonged to the Palace of Versailles. Previously, the luxury hotel had served as the French headquarters of the *Luftwaffe*, commanded by the Sun King of the Third Reich, *Reichsmarschall* Hermann Göring.[2]

This Christmas, special instructions were issued here pertaining to a special operation that had taken place on the ground as well in the air. In a whimsical article, entitled "Censors Reveal Details of Blitz by Gen S. Claus," journalist Larry Rue reported that SHAEF (Supreme Headquarters Allied Expeditionary Forces) had proclaimed that "a new North Pole command has been formed" led by Santa Claus, who had a small ground army of gnomes at his disposal. The Allied censors prohibited any speculation as to the exact location of Santa's headquarters as well as "any estimate as to strength and equipment of the army of gnomes." As to the aerial operation, it was forbidden to write about which "scientific techniques" would be used to drop parcels into chimneys. Code names like Thunder, Lightning, etc. were off limits, and estimates about "speed, range and load carrying capacity of reindeer" were also prohibited.[3]

On Christmas Day, Ike sat down to dinner with a number of confidants, but according to his driver and private secretary, Kay Summersby, he was not in a cheerful mood. Since May 1942, when she first met him, she had never seen him so depressed or so dejected.[4] The reason for this may have been the rumor that the Germans were planning an attempt on his life, although one can assume that the unexpected German offensive in the Ardennes caused him great concern. Whatever the case, he could not display any of this somberness during an informal meeting that probably took place before Christmas Day in an army camp with a carefully selected group of representatives of the Allied forces in Europe. Both Americans and British from army, navy and air force were present, as well as two French from the Free French Forces. It was remarkable that, in a time in which racism was still an acceptable phenomenon, an African-American soldier was present as well. A report in a British news reel showed Eisenhower clumsily driving up in his jeep, as he generally was driven by Summersby. He conveyed his Christmas wishes to all members of the mixed group of soldiers, who would all be asked to deliver a Christmas message to the citizens of their own countries. "This is the best Christmas we've seen yet," Eisenhower said in encouragement, "and let's hope that when the next one comes around, we can all be back with our own people."[5]

Away from the Ardennes, many of Eisenhower's compatriots also spent their Christmas of this war year in a foreign country. Not so far away from the battlegrounds of the Ardennes offensive, near the French town of Bitche in the Vosges, Joseph Farris had a quiet Christmas. When the Japanese attacked Pearl Harbor, he was still in high school. It wasn't until 1943 that he, age 18, was drafted into the army. He was assigned to the 100th Infantry Division as a foot soldier and was transferred to Europe in October 1944. He got his baptism by fire in the Vosges in November. In December he and his unit were involved in heavy fighting in the capture of the Maginot line near Bitche. While taking Freudenberg Fortress on higher ground, the unit had suffered a high number of casualties caused by the ferocious German defense from bunkers. These bunkers had to be knocked out one by one by the Americans, who were subjected to German artillery barrages in the nearly impenetrable hilly terrain. After the fortress had been captured and turned into a battalion command post, the division had to take up defensive positions instead of continuing their advance. This was because the Ardennes offensive now claimed all attention. In the days prior to Christmas, Farris's battalion was able to recover after 16 men were killed and 120 wounded during the battle for Bitche.[6] For this action, the battalion was awarded a Presidential Unit Citation.[7]

Recuperating from the fighting earlier that month, Farris wrote a letter to his parents on December 23rd, indicating he thought very much of home, "especially because it is so near to our greatest day of the year. I'd give a million dollars to be home with you all but that's being selfish on my part because there are so many other boys in the same predicament. Many of them haven't been home in a couple of years while I saw you all about three months ago." On Christmas Eve, he only had the company of a mate with whom he shared his foxhole. Around them lay an "eerily quiet landscape – cold, snowy and dark." They whispered Merry Christmas to each other while they were looking out for an invisible enemy, located somewhere in the dark, who did not have a merry Christmas either. "The night was uneventful, and [I] spent much of it thinking of home and parents and two brothers," Farris declared later. "What was I doing here? I was feeling sorry for myself. I had been lucky in combat so far. ... I always feared what might come next. Each new day had me wondering if today there would be a bullet or shell with my name on it."[8]

On Christmas Day, the young soldier wrote another letter home in which he wished his family a "belated Merry Christmas to you all." He told them that he and the other boys had set up a small Christmas tree and adorned it with trinkets that one of them had taken from a nearby house. "And to top it all," Farris continued, "we decided something was still missing so we wound up some toilet paper around it. You'd be surprised how much better it looks with the toilet paper – you can leave that to the ingenuity of the Yankees." Lacking presents, they laid a machine gun under the tree.

For them, Christmas Day was a lot better than for most of their colleagues in the Ardennes. They had "a fine Christmas dinner" with "plenty of turkey, potatoes, peas, carrots, cranberry sauce, cocoa, mince pie, two cans of beer, candy and a cigar," followed by a movie.[9] After the Christmas holidays, there was still enough to eat such as donuts and tinned spaghetti. In the last days of December they enjoyed a period of rest in a small village where life proceeded as "something out of the past," according to Farris. The villagers still used ancient tools, wore wooden shoes and kept themselves warm with wood stoves. Since he had not gone to church on Christmas, he made up for it on December 31. Meanwhile, the snow was thick on the ground. "Everything looks nice and peaceful outside, except for the occasional roar of big guns," he wrote in a letter home on December 31.[10]

Also in France, but far away from the enemy front, Sergeant Betty Maguson Olson was in Paris in December 1944. A member of the Women's Army Corps (WAC), she had been stationed in the French capital since September 1944 with the 29th Traffic Regulating Group, responsible for directing traffic in streets full of military vehicles. On December 16, she had a foretaste of Christmas when someone at the office distributed chocolate ice cream, something she had not had for six months. She and her colleague Berta also received a Normandy apple tart from their commanding general, which she shared with the men at the office. Although Christmas decorations had already been put up, she was not yet in a Christmas mood. "Most of us are just glad we work on Christmas Day since then there won't be any chance for sitting around thinking about what's doing at home," she wrote. Nevertheless they took a lot of trouble to create a Christmas atmosphere at the office. "Our Day Rooms both look very Christmassy now," Olson declared. "One has a big tree and one a little one. Of course, they aren't like a modern American tree – things are hand-made like popcorn chains. It's really attractive though. And there is mistletoe up practically everywhere in the hotel entrance and in all the halls at the office. The boys say they are going to put some in the elevators too!"

On Christmas Eve, she wrote in a letter to her family that she assumed that "the recent war news has more or less put a damper on a really 'merry' Christmas at home too," referring, of course, to the Ardennes offensive. She reported to the home front that it was cold in Paris but there was no snow and she had received her Christmas gifts sent from the U.S. In addition, a colonel from the Office of the Chief of Transportation had delighted her and Berta with a small bottle each of "wonderful perfume." "And then – ssh – we were also given a bottle of champagne, so we are going to sneak (!) it into our billets and have a bit of a party! Hm – I'll bet you think Paris has corrupted me, but champagne over here is in about the same class as lemonade back home." (In an answer to her letter, her father voiced his concern about the champagne, and in a subsequent letter she assured him that she would never drink more than three glasses and that the stuff was little more than a soft drink.) Early evening she took part in a Christmas sing-along under the Arc de Triomphe, but she experienced it as a total flop. Afterwards she attended services in the American cathedral where some WACs joined the regular choir. The church was packed with soldiers, but some civilians also attended. "Two little old ladies" were sitting next to Olson; one of them told her the other one had been in hiding for the past two years, so this was very special Christmas for her.

After the service, Olson and her colleagues were met outside the cathedral by trucks and driven – under guard because of the Ardennes offensive – to the General Hospital where they went on to sing old-fashioned Christmas carols for the American soldiers who had been admitted there. En route, they warmed themselves up by singing classic songs like "Jingle Bells." The sick and wounded soldiers were highly pleased by the visit of the women. "They'd insist on all the girls coming in the various wards," according to Olson, "so they could see us all, and several of the more energetic ones chased a WAC or two down the hall with a piece of mistletoe. We'd keep picking up fellows who were well able to walk. ... They all wanted 'White Christmas' over and over again. We sang so much and so hard that we were all hoarse when we got done. We could tell they all enjoyed it very much, and they all thanked us so. ... We agreed it was the very best way to spend Christmas Eve." Back in the hotel, she, Berta and another friend threw their own party. They drank the captain's champagne and had cocktail crackers, sliced olives and fruit cake.

The next morning, Christmas Day, started with a breakfast at which Olson and her colleagues had fresh eggs for the first time since their departure from the United States. Officers and N.C.O.s doubled as cooks and waiters. That day the American again wrote to her family to let them know, "We've really had a very nice Christmas." Her best present had been the headlines in the army paper *Stars and Stripes* – in particular "Yanks stop Nazi attack." She had been working on Christmas Day, and in the streets compatriots repeatedly wished her a Merry Christmas. From jeeps passing by, the boys called out "Merry Christmas, Sarge" or "Merry Christmas WACie."

She was proud that "in the midst of a war which we're very close to, and without any Christmas atmosphere except that we make ourselves," Americans could still keep up a Christmas spirit. It became a real feast when a dumbfounded Olson received a Christmas present from her general, a wristwatch, just like the rest of the office staff. After Christmas was over, the young woman attended a performance of *Romeo and Juliet* on December 30 in the Grand Opera, but because the building was unheated, she was unable to wear an evening dress. In a letter from her parents which she received on January 2nd, she was informed about the latest war victims in her suburb, which brought her back to harsh reality.[11]

This Christmas, journalist Walter Cronkite was busier than during the previous two. Shortly after the start of the Ardennes offensive he was called to Paris to help out in the busy office of the United Press. Although he had been looking forward to a holiday celebration in the

French capital, he had left for the front on Christmas Eve. Despite the cold, he was dressed in his normal clothing. Other items – long Johns, boots, gloves and a leather coat – he could not obtain before January 3rd, 1945. He worked for four days nonstop, but he judged he had little success as there were other journalists present who were better than himself. To his regret, it was only on December 27 that he managed to write a letter to his wife, telling her he had had an "awfully lonely Christmas – the worst ever, I think. I must admit that the surroundings weren't too unpleasant, but the fact that I was alone again without you made it almost unbearable." He spent Christmas Day in the city of Luxembourg which he described as "just as lovely as the post cards." At night he had a turkey dinner, along with Ernest Hemingway, Martha Gellhorn and other journalists. "We had some eggnog and everyone else, except old hard-working Cronkite, who had a fistful of mediocre stories to do, got pretty well pied. I had a few drinks and filed my last story about midnight after which I was so tired I just collapsed into bed."[12]

Walter Cronkite and his colleagues in Luxembourg had no idea that on Christmas Eve, a tragedy unfolded off the Normandy coast that would be kept under lock and key by the American army until 1959. The disaster took place in the English Channel where the Belgian troop transport vessel *Léopoldville* was on its way from Southampton in Great Britain to the European continent. The ship carried 2,223 American soldiers of the 66th Infantry Division who were to strengthen the forces in the Ardennes. The steamer, built in 1929, had been used for luxury cruises before the war, but nothing of that could be seen. Anything considered superfluous was removed in order to carry more passengers. Nevertheless, the vessel with 2,223 soldiers and a crew of 237 was overcrowded,[13] especially in the hold where soldiers made the journey, lying in hammocks and sitting at picnic tables in the passageways. "The stench aboard was really intense," passenger Vincent Codianni recalls. "Down below we were packed like sardines in a tin."[14] Far away from home on Christmas Eve, in heavy seas en route to a war zone, the spirit aboard was tense and depressed. If it wasn't fear or nostalgia the men felt, it was sea sickness. In these circumstances the trip was far from pleasant, but it would get much worse.

Somewhere near the Belgian vessel, the German *U-486*, commanded by *Kapitän* Gerhard Meyer, was lying in wait for prey. Aboard, the U-boat's cook had made all preparations for Christmas.

"He had baked a pie for everyone," according to a crew member. "The cream had been whipped. ... We had good food. We were ready for Christmas."[15] Suddenly all men were called to their battle stations. A convoy, including the *Léopoldville*, was spotted. Sinking an Allied ship justified postponing the Christmas celebration. Aboard the Belgian vessel, there was hardly any Christmas spirit. Despite the cold, some 20 soldiers had opted to leave the hold to sing Christmas carols in the fresh air on deck. To avoid being spotted by the enemy the vessel was darkened. The lights of Cherbourg, the ship's destination, were blinking in the distance, making the men feel at ease now that the journey would soon be over.[16] Suddenly, passengers and crew were shocked by a massive bang. In the hold, men were flung from their hammocks, and the crew called to them in Flemish to come up on deck.[17] Meanwhile, the U-boat that had fired the torpedo which struck the *Léopoldville* amidships descended to the seabed where she remained unseen and safe from depth charges.

As the freezing sea water rushed in below deck, everything that could go wrong did go wrong aboard the vessel. Panic broke out and the men had to struggle to get out of the ship's hold. Once on deck, they made the terrible discovery that the crew had already abandoned ship with all of the lifeboats, of which far too few had been aboard. Swimming vests were not available in sufficient numbers and safety instructions had not been given.[18] "I heard all kinds of yelling," Ed Phillips later declared about the situation on board. "I heard many boys calling for their mother. I did so too because the one person I really cared about was my mother."[19] Some men plunged into the freezing water while others jumped aboard the H.M.S. *Brilliant*, one of the escorts which had come alongside the *Léopoldville*. Hank Anderson, who had directed the singing of the Christmas carols on deck, watched some men stiffen at the prospect of having to jump. "These guys were paralyzed. They just would not jump. And they had seen some jump, and not made it. So it was quite a jump across. And I remember getting over there and sliding across what little deck there was, slammed into the bulwark that was there; staggered back up to the rail. And the sight that I had made it enabled them then to start jumping." He was safe but others misjudged their jump, landed between the vessels and were crushed.[20]

The *Léopoldville* sank around 20:45. Some 500 men had managed to board H.M.S. *Brilliant* safely while others still floated in the water. One of them was Ed Phillips who had to beat off several men to prevent him from going under. He was to be picked up by one of the vessels that had come to the rescue from Cherbourg, a mere 6.5 miles away.[21] Through miscommunication, the rescue operation had gotten under way far too late, resulting in numerous unnecessary victims.

Hank Anderson, who attributed his survival partly to the fact that he had left the hold to sing Christmas carols, told how he and the other survivors were taken care of in Cherbourg by black soldiers. "They surrounded us and sang Christmas carols. And I, I was so stunned."[22] A total of nearly 800 Americans would lose their lives either from drowning aboard the vessel, from hypothermia or from injuries sustained after they had jumped overboard. Captain Charles Limbor went down with his vessel too. A Belgian crew member and three Congolese also lost their lives.[23] This was not only a personal tragedy for passengers, crew and their next of kin but also a painful loss for the American war effort, yearning for reinforcements to be deployed in the Ardennes. Many of the rescued men were no longer fit for duty but had to recuperate in French hospitals from hypothermia or injuries.

Unaware of the sinking of the *Léopoldville*, American military personnel shared the festivities with civilians in various locations in Europe. In Savere in Alsace, liberated for the most part in November 1944 by American and French troops, Private First Class Peter Feyen played Santa Claus for 150 children, mostly orphans. Although he was in his usual battledress and he had a three-day stubble instead of a long white beard, the candy he distributed was no less tasty for the boys and girls who had not celebrated Christmas for four years. Men from his liaison unit with the air force had given the local youth their chocolate rations and candy from their Christmas parcels. In addition, they had brought toys from Paris and oranges from North Africa to hand out. "Some of the youngsters had never seen an orange before and weren't quite certain whether to eat the fruit or bounce it," reporter Seymour Korman wrote. The children experienced another first by watching a Mickey Mouse movie. The mayor of the village expressed his gratitude for what the Americans had done and added that the Germans had never made a gesture like that during the occupation.[24]

Oranges also played an important role in the recollections of Christmas 1944 of 1st Lieutenant Robert J. Fisher. Posted to the 544th Bomb Squadron, 384th Bomb Group, he was stationed at R.A.F. Grafton Underwood. He and his bombardier had been invited to Christmas dinner by an English family in their home in Northampton, 25 miles southeast of the base. As he did not want to come empty-handed, for a few days beforehand he and his mate each set aside the orange that came with their breakfast. Some of their friends donated their oranges too; so eventually they had collected some fifteen oranges as a hostess gift. When they handed the bag of oranges to their grateful hostess, she immediately put all but two or three of them into a beautiful bowl which she placed on the mantelpiece. She and her husband next peeled the oranges she had kept apart. "The lady then asked her husband to go get the neighborhood children and bring them over to the house," Fisher said years later. "When the children arrived, the wife and her husband gave each child a section or two to eat and let them smell and feel the peeling. We thought this a little strange and asked them why they did it that way. They explained that they just had to share with the neighborhood children because most of them had never even seen an orange before, let alone tasted one!" Fisher was happy his present had been received so well. He was pleased "to witness an outstanding example of the true Christmas spirit. I will never forget Christmas of 1944."[25]

In Paris, the Americans distributed champagne and cognac among the citizens. In their haste to leave town, the Germans had left thousands of cases of these beverages behind. For many of the youngest children in France this was the first time they celebrated Christmas after an occupation of four years. Over those years, their parents had had neither opportunity nor means to celebrate Christmas.[26]

Nicole, about eight years old, did not know what Christmas was all about either. She was the daughter of the resistance couple with whom 20-year-old soldier Vernon Alexander from Arkansas and his mate Paul had moved in. Alexander was a machine gunner in the 2nd Battalion, 411th Regiment. In the French village where his unit had been quartered he had selected the small family house as their shelter because it had a large bay window which offered a clear view of any Germans who might approach. Communication between the French and the Americans proceeded laboriously as they did not speak each other's language. The Frenchman, Nicolas, was recuperating from a groin injury he had sustained from an exploding grenade, and his wife Lucy was afraid of what might still be in store for her family. For yet another year, a somber Christmas awaited their little daughter, but the Americans refused to let that happen. "She needed an American Christmas," Vernon stated years later.

After Nicole had tasted chocolate for the first time thanks to the Americans, Vernon and Paul now went out of their way to let her celebrate a real Christmas. She had not experienced this before or she could not remember it. They left the safety of the village to cut down a tree which they decorated with garlands made with wrapping paper from parcels from the USA. In their camp they found two dolls which they wrapped up for the girl. For Nicole's father, who was risking his life sheltering Americans, they found a box of cigars and tobacco. While Paul distracted the mess sergeant, Vernon stole fried ham, flour, sugar and some fruit from the mess tent. They smuggled the food and the Christmas tree into the home of the French family.

The next morning, about a week before Christmas, when Nicole saw the tree with the presents under it, she shrieked with joy. Her mother used the food from the mess to prepare a delicious holiday dinner. "We had ourselves a Christmas dinner and it was absolutely tops," Vernon said. "Little Nicole was beside herself. She had never had a doll before." The little girl's joy distracted the soldiers from the war which still had many horrors in store. A few months later, Vernon Alexander would witness the liberation of concentration camps. After the war, the images of stacks of emaciated corpses would often haunt him, but he cherished the memory of Nicole's first Christmas.[27]

At the front in Italy, the Allied advance was held up by heavy snowfall on Christmas Day.[28] Rome had been liberated on June 4, 1944, by the Americans. In the city on December 24, the Pope, in his Christmas speech, advocated democracy and unity among all nations. He called for punishment of the aggressor within the framework of justice. For the first time since the year 800, civilians were admitted to the Christmas celebration in the basilica of St. Peter, where the façade could be illuminated again since the blackout had been lifted. With 75,000 visitors, including many military, the space was so overcrowded that some soldiers climbed onto confessional boxes to be able to watch the service.[29] Members of the Swiss Guard sang "Silent Night" in German.[30]

A little less than 250 miles northeast of the Italian capital in the picturesque Tuscany village of Barga, a platoon of some 60 soldiers celebrated Christmas with the civilian population. They were members of the 92nd Infantry Division, a segregated unit of African-American soldiers, also known as the Buffalo soldiers after the image of a buffalo on their divisional badges. On Christmas Eve, they distributed a truck load of various food stuffs, including chocolate and cheese. "We had never seen so much food," Irma Biondi – at the time 17 years of age – recalled. "They were wonderful, so nice to us. My little brother followed them like shadows."

Something like four or five soldiers were invited to a Christmas dinner by the family of the then 12-year-old Tullio Bertini. He and his parents had been born in the U.S. and were visiting Italy, but due to the outbreak of war they had not been able to return. Because of their mutual nationality, the soldiers felt at home with the Bertinis. As mother Bertini and a neighbor prepared dinner, the soldiers had brought a number of records with American dance music and a record player. "We had the dinner," Tullio recalled; "the soldiers mellowed by drinking wine, played music, danced with my mother. ... I thought it seemed the soldiers felt like they were in America, and I also think that my father and mother felt the same way, perhaps thinking that soon we would go back to the United States. The color of their skin did not come into focus. I thought they were Allied soldiers who had come to help get the Italians out of the WW II mess."

The pleasant evening was disrupted because German and Italian soldiers – fighting for Mussolini's puppet government and dressed in civilian clothes – infiltrated Barga and surrounding villages. The next day, a German-Italian offensive was launched during which some 40 African-Americans were killed. Barga was captured by the enemy but was recaptured by the Allies just a week later.[31]

Although more than one million African-Americans were fighting under the same flag and against the same enemy, this did not safeguard them against racism. They were discriminated against by both the army leadership and the white soldiers. As a result, the vast majority of black soldiers were in supporting roles like drivers or cooks and were housed in camps separated from their white colleagues. Their officers were mostly white, and fighting alongside white soldiers was out of the question. In the southern states of the U.S., it was not uncommon practice that German POWs received better treatment than their black guards, but they had to contend with racism in the northern states as well. In Detroit, 2,600 white workers went on strike in 1943 in protest against the employment of African-American workers in their factory. "I'd rather see Hitler and Hirohito win the war than work beside a nigger on the assembly line!" one protester shouted, using the insulting racial epithet.[32]

On the island of Guam, recaptured on August 10, 1944, racial tensions got completely out of hand during the Christmas holidays. The incident, which initially was suppressed by the authorities, also came to be known as the third battle for Guam. The first battle took place in 1941 with the Japanese invasion and the second in 1944 when the Americans recaptured the island.[33]

The race riots arose from the presence of African-American personnel on official leave in the town of Agana. Although severely damaged during bombardments by the American navy, the largest city on the island was a spot where servicemen could relax and make contact with local females. The fact that African-American servicemen did likewise did not go well with some white Marines of the 3rd Marine Division. "And as in the United States, sexual jealousy and rivalry played an major role in fostering racial conflict," civil rights activist Francis White concluded. He visited the island shortly after Christmas to investigate the incident. "Many of the Americans, particularly Southern-born Marines, bitterly resented the sight of a Negro talking to a female Guamanian."[34] Small gangs of Marines started turning away African-American Navy personnel by force.[35] Things did not end there because Marines in passing trucks started throwing rocks and smoke canisters into the camp of their African-American countrymen. Complaints about this by African-Americans were usually hushed up, although the Provost Marshall on the island did declare in mid-December that discrimination by reason of age group, race, religion or political beliefs was prohibited.[36]

In spite of the urgent appeal of the Provost Marshall, on Christmas Eve a group of African-Americans celebrating in Agana was fired upon by white Marines and chased out of the city. As a rumor circulated to the effect that one of their mates had been shot by the Marines, a large group of black servicemen wanted revenge. The Military Police managed to stop them, and the return of the missing comrade defused the atmosphere. Later a gang of white Marines arrived in the camp shortly after midnight. A chunk of coral was allegedly thrown at one of their colleagues who was injured as a result. A white officer managed to prevent things getting out of hand. On Christmas Day, things got worse though as an African-American was shot to death by white Marines. Another African-American – according to Walter White – was seriously injured later in the day after having been shot by a white sailor.[37] According to some other sources however, that day a white American had been killed by an African-American compatriot.[38] In any case, that night the African-American camp was strafed by machine gun fire from a jeep. The fire was returned but the gunner escaped. A white Military Police officer was injured after having been shot by African-American men eager for retribution. A group of forty of them, armed with bats and knives, boarded a truck to go to Agana to get revenge but were stopped at a road block. They were all arrested and sentenced to prison terms, although this punishment was reversed after the protest of Walter Francis White.[39] Some white people as well were punished for their contribution to the conflict.[40]

African-Americans performing supporting duties at the nuclear research facility in Hanford, Washington, were not spared discrimination either. Apart from being housed in a separate part of the camp, they were also excluded from the celebrations of their white coworkers. While all kinds of shows, sports games, dance nights and circus acts were organized for whites from mid-December until New Year's, for the African-American workers there were only simple activities like card games and bingo.[41]

In the race against Germany to develop a war-ending atomic bomb, there really was something to celebrate on Christmas Day 1944: in the U.S., the first radioactive slugs of fissionable material were discharged from B Reactor at the Hanford Site in Washington State. After a few weeks in storage, they were transferred by rail to a chemical facility some 9 miles away. The plutonium was further purified, and the first shipment of high grade plutonium was sent in early February 1945 to Los Alamos, New Mexico, where the atom bomb was being developed.[42]

In Los Alamos, similarly sealed off from the outside world, a number of military personnel from a scientific department of the army and a few WACs gathered in the auditorium this Christmas to hear a speech by General Lesley R. Groves, the military head of the Manhattan project. As he boasted to the women that they had to keep their eyes peeled because this was probably the nearest they could get to a general, he urged only the men to write home during Christmas "even if you put your name on a piece of paper and put it in an envelope."[43] When he asked if there were any questions or ideas, only one man spoke up. He suggested baseball gloves, bats and balls, and the general promised to look into it.[44]

In other places in the U.S. and elsewhere, entertainment during the holidays was provided for the American troops. There was bad news, though, for those who had been looking forward to seeing Glenn Miller perform with his Army Air Force Band. On December 24, the American press wrote that the major and bandleader had been reported missing.[45] During the flight from England to Paris, his single engine plane had crashed on December 15. Neither the wreckage nor the remains of the pilot, Miller and a fellow passenger were ever found, and the exact cause of the crash has never been clarified. On Christmas morning, a memorial service was held in La Madeleine Church. Both in the afternoon and in the evening, the band played in the Olympia Hall to a rapturous audience paying tribute to the great artist.[46]

Another American icon who had traveled to Europe to entertain the troops captured the hearts of both Allied and German troops with her sex appeal and her rendition of the song "Lili Marlene." In many army barracks, there was a pin-up picture of her looking seductively into the camera lens. Born in Germany, movie star and singer Marlene Dietrich performed for the Allies in Italy and western Europe. She made herself popular with the men by being close to them: she ate the same food, wore the same uniform and performed close to the battle zones. Despite her frequent drinks of Calvados to keep warm, traveling along the front that winter exacted its toll. In her memoirs, she called Christmas 1944 sad, also because she was plagued by lice. "We all felt down, exhausted. It was becoming harder for us to perform with the same enthusiasm as before."[47]

Multi-talented Bob Hope was also very popular among the troops. Born in England as Leslie Townes Hope, he – at four years of age – had emigrated to the U.S. with his parents in 1903. Starting as a vaudeville artist, he later gained much success under his professional name Bob Hope with his whimsical show on NBC radio. In 1941 he hosted his show for the first time outside the studio before an audience of thousands of military personnel. He was delighted with the enthusiasm and spontaneity of the public. It marked the beginning of a series of radio broadcasts from army and navy bases in the U.S. and tours along the front. Only nine out of his 144 radio shows during the war were recorded in the NBC studios. He always started his shows with "This is Bob ____ Hope," replacing the blank with the name of the base. In 1942, he became the master of ceremonies of the Hollywood Victory Caravan, a two-week tour through American cities with 50 Hollywood stars including Bing Crosby and Stan Laurel and Oliver Hardy (Laurel & Hardy), which yielded over $700,000 dollars for army and navy relief funds. This was followed by 65 shows at military facilities and hospitals. That year, Hope also performed for the first time with the USO, the United Service Organizations, established in 1941 by request of President Roosevelt, that provided entertainment for the troops. Many USO shows were to follow including in Alaska, England, North-Africa, Italy and the Pacific. Time and again, Hope and his sidekicks were enthusiastically received by the troops. He himself had a sound explanation for his success: "The reason for our overwhelming reception by troops the world over, was that we, more than anything else, sounded like home."[48]

Hope's show of December 23, 1944 was broadcast both from the NBC's Hollywood studio and then from a merchant marine ship – a Liberty ship – on the west coast. "This is Bob Hope speaking to you from Hollywood," he started his show. "Did you ever hear of Z-men? Sounds like a gag, doesn't it? Well, it isn't. Z-men are the guys without whom General 'Ike's' army and Admiral Nimitz's navy couldn't live. Five thousand seven hundred of them have died from enemy torpedoes, mines, bombs or bullets since our zero hour at Pearl Harbor."

The men he was talking about were the crews of the American merchant fleet who took their nickname from their identification papers, also known as Z-cards. Of all American services, these men ran the greatest risk of dying in the course of their duties. A total of some 9,300 of them would lose their lives during the war.[49] Hope emphasized that these men worked for minimum wages in dangerous situations. Some of them "labored in a hot engine room, never knowing when a torpedo might smash the hull above you and send thousands of tons of sea water in to snuff out your life." As an example of the courage of the merchant mariners, he mentioned Sailor Joe Squires and Engineer Hal Whitney who lost their lives aboard the S.S. *Maiden Creek* on March 17, 1944, lowering the life boats after their vessel had been struck by a torpedo.[50]

Hope mentioned the amount of 70 million tons of freight which had been delivered to the various fronts by the merchant fleet in 1944. "These boys won't be in the United States for Christmas," Hope said, "so the USS – United Seamen's Service – is providing them with an early Christmas party which we're all invited to attend." Next, NBC reporter Val Brown took over from the bridge of a Liberty ship berthed somewhere on the American west coast ready for departure to the Pacific. The crew had gathered around him. A Santa Claus distributed gifts. A pole, 15 feet tall with red, green and white signal lights on the tips of the yards, served as a substitute for a Christmas tree.

The reporter had Hope talk to a number of crew members, such as a navy gunner who had spent 15 days in a lifeboat and the second cook, who said that the Christmas dinner included turkey, mashed potatoes, green peas with cream sauce, cranberry sauce, celery, hot rolls, hot mince pie and coffee. The program ended with a choir singing "O Come All Ye Faithful" as they were taken by motorboat around the harbor alongside various vessels. After Santa Claus had been hoisted off the ship, a whistle sounded and she set sail to deliver the cargo. Bob Hope wished the crew "Bon Voyage. ... Merry Christmas to you and to all the merchant seamen, wherever this Christmas finds you! Merry Christmas everyone."[51]

In the Pacific Theatre of Operations, General MacArthur had fulfilled his promise, made in 1942, to return to the Philippine islands. During the battles in the Philippine Sea on June 19 and 20 and in the Gulf of Leyte October 23-26, 1944, heavy losses had been inflicted on the Japanese navy and air force. On October 20, the Americans went ashore on Leyte, one of the larger islands in the Philippines. General MacArthur had his picture taken while wading through the surf on the heels of his troops and stepping onto Philippine soil in wet trousers. While the American navy was being harassed by Kamikaze attacks, MacArthur's troops, including Philippine guerilla fighters, fought their way inland, continuously thwarted by fierce Japanese resistance, heavy typhoon rains and suicide attacks. It would take until December 26 before the entire island was captured although Japanese guerilla attacks continued afterwards.[52]

MacArthur celebrated Christmas in Tacloban, the capital of the province of Leyte which had been recaptured by American and Philippines troops shortly after the invasion. He had taken up residence in a luxurious mansion that had belonged to a rich compatriot. A group of soldiers assembled on Christmas Eve in front of the house to sing Christmas carols. The sound of low flying Japanese fighters put an abrupt end to the singing. The dark sky was illuminated by the fast-moving beams of searchlights. Anti-aircraft guns managed to shoot down one of the aircraft.[53]

Apparently, neither money nor effort were spared to provide MacArthur's men in the Philippines with turkey and gifts from home.

Hundreds of high priority mail bags containing Christmas gifts had taken more than a week before they could be received by soldiers and navy personnel. A refrigerator vessel delivered 1 million pounds of turkey which was distributed among the men. The *Chicago Tribune* wrote on December 24: "By airplane, fast boat, land vehicles, and on the backs of carabaos and men, the turkey is going to the front lines." In order to wash down the poultry, beer was also distributed between Christmas Eve and New Year's Day. According to a major who was involved in the distribution, the turkeys, previously prepared in mess kitchens, would even be delivered, if necessary, to the most distant foxholes, so that no one would be left out. Transport aircraft of the U.S. Pacific Fleet also distributed decorated Christmas trees to the troops in the tropics, from the Solomon Islands to Saipan, "bringing something of a home touch to sailors at lonely island outposts." The vessels of the fleet in Pearl Harbor and recreational facilities on the island received their Christmas trees as well.[54] Some two months later, on the island of Iwo Jima, a new costly battle awaited many of the men who had celebrated a relatively quiet Christmas 1944.

Back in the U.S., two Christmas songs were written in 1944 which to this day are still played on radio during the Christmas season. Although the official title of one of these is "The Christmas Song," it became better known by its opening line, "Chestnuts Roasting on an Open Fire." The song was written and composed on a stiflingly hot summer day in the house of song writer Robert Wells, who had returned from service in the air force. "It was so damn hot," Wells explained later, "I thought I'd write something to cool myself off. All I could think of was Christmas and cold weather." As he was mixing words that pertained to Christmas, composer Mel Tormé – who had graduated from high school a year before – sat at the piano. Within 45 minutes they had completed the nostalgic song, but it would take until 1946 before it was produced and released, sung by Nat King Cole.[55]

Another equally great Christmas hit was "Have Yourself a Merry Little Christmas" written by Hugh Martin and Ralph Blaine. Judy Garland sang the comforting song in the 1944 movie *Meet Me in St. Louis* to her character's sister, who was sad because their father wanted to move the family to New York. The lyrics of the song promised better times and were therefore highly applicable to the current situation.

50

"Next year all our troubles will be out of sight" was a promise millions of Americans would have loved to see fulfilled.[56]

It was not a happy Christmas in the U.S. More Americans than ever had been sent overseas to the front. Since D-Day on June 6, 1944, thousands of them had been killed or wounded. In addition to living rooms at the home front being decorated with Christmas wreaths and mistletoe, increasingly more small flags with gold, silver or blue stars were hung in windows. A blue star meant that a family member had been sent overseas for military service, the silver star meant that a family member had been wounded, and the gold star meant someone had been killed in action.[57] Although rationing was far less stringent than in Europe, home cooks had to use margarine for the first time during Christmas instead of real butter, and for example sugar, meat, cooking oil and canned goods were rationed as well.[58] Asked what people wanted for Christmas the vast majority of responses included the end of the war and the return of fathers and sons.[59]

In order to feel connected with their next of kin overseas, this year Christmas greetings were once more massively exchanged through V-mail, the military mail using micro film. During the war, 1.5 million messages would be transmitted though this medium.[60] If someone wanted to send flowers from the front to his mother, wife or girlfriend, he could make use of "flowers by wire" whereby flowers could be ordered by headquarters radio communication to the U.S. and then be delivered to the address desired.[61]

While in many European countries, the sending of Christmas cards decreased sharply, this was not the case in the U.S. Not that there wasn't a shortage of paper: because of the draft, the timber industry suffered a shortage of workers (the supply of Christmas trees was just enough in 1944[62]), and too little wood pulp was reaching the paper mills. Recycling was the solution however. "Every scrap of paper, every piece of cardboard of your Christmas wrappings should be salvaged and turned in to make new paper and cardboard for our forces," *Life Magazine* wrote on December 25, 1944. The army needed it for packing and wrapping ammunition, food stuffs, blood plasma, medicines and other supplies.[63] After the attack on Pearl Harbor, the War Department had initially ordered a reduction of the use of paper, which severely reduced the release of Christmas cards. A group of publishers successfully protested against this. To meet the army half way, the group launched projects benefitting the war effort, such as campaigns to buy defense stamps, the profits of which flowed into the funds of the War Department.

Consumers could collect the stamps and later exchange them for government war bonds.[64]

Post cards with various themes were released for the home front, but the American flag or its colors were often depicted. Uncle Sam, the Statue of Liberty and other characteristic American symbols were also frequently seen. Humorous and cartoon-like images of GIs were popular, as were funny drawings of Santa Claus exchanging his sleigh for an army jeep or a military aircraft. Cards were tailored for mothers, wives, girlfriends and other senders. Special post cards were printed by divisions and other army or navy units. They depicted, for instance, divisional badges or the vessel the sender sailed on. Servicemen could send post cards from Paris showing the Eiffel Tower flying the American flag and depicting other points of interest in the French capital.[65]

A Christmas card American servicemen and women could send to the home front from Paris in 1944.

The enemy also turned to the American military with post cards. The Japanese for instance had already distributed seven different cards in 1942 during the battle for Guadalcanal, four of them depicting a pin-up girl with beautiful legs. The text had allegedly been written by a wife at home and was meant to evoke home sickness.[66] The Germans took it a step further by distributing a Christmas message during the Ardennes offensive, suggesting to the GIs to return to the U.S. slightly wounded or sick. "Christmas in the States? Well? Why not?" the message reads, which was accompanied by an image and description of a traditional Christmas celebration in the U.S. with "roasted pork, cranberry sauce, mashed potatoes, gravy and meat pie, the best ever."[67]

Apart from publishers of post cards, other American enterprises adapted to the Christmas holidays in war time. This was obvious for instance from the ads in *Life Magazine*. During the first years of the war, these ads were often of a somber nature. "We shall ride this storm through!" watchmaker Hamilton assured the public in 1942 with a drawing of the Statue of Liberty shrouded in dark clouds. An accompanying text explained that this year only a limited supply of watches was available as the company was busy producing precision instruments for the army.[68] In the same year, Texaco pictured a sad Dutch farmer with the text: "Patience, Pieter, patience..." The company that delivered fuel to the armed forces promised that the Dutchman would have to wait just a little longer. "Our [fighting] machine is almost ready... almost ready to help sweep that evil machine from your country, from Europe, from the good green earth... forever." Also in 1942, General Electric launched a double-page ad with a sad-looking girl next to a Christmas tree with the accompanying text: "The Light no war will ever dim."[69]

In contrast with peacetime ad messages, many wartime ads called for thriftiness. In 1943, the American Meat Institute urged consumers not to waste any meat. Even the last drop of gravy had to be eaten during Christmas dinner.[70] Other organizations were eager to let the consumer know how they contributed to the war effort. That same year, Curtiss Wright Corporation placed an ad explaining how an aircraft manufacturer producing transport aircraft contributed to the delivery of blood plasma to field hospitals. An illustration is shown of a young soldier whose life is being saved by "wise" surgeons in an open air field hospital with a blinking star in the sky, an unmistakable reference to the Christmas story.[71]

From 1944 on, the ads grew more optimistic in nature. They had already been printed prior to the Ardennes offensive on the assumption that an Allied victory was imminent. Coca Cola placed a particularly cheerful ad (Have a "Coke" = Merry Christmas) in the form of an illustration of a cozy living room with a Christmas tree, where a few soldiers and their family were celebrating. It was probably the dream of many Americans in the armed forces but far from reality for many.[72] Chocolate manufacturer Whitman's placed a joyous ad as well, depicting a woman dressed as Santa Claus with a picture of her husband in uniform on her dressing table.[73]

Car manufacturer Studebaker placed an ad with a more traditional vision of Christmas. Beneath an image of an illuminated church in a snowy landscape, a serious text included: "Mankind again will live with dignity and pride in the clean atmosphere of triumph over tyranny."[74] Manufacturer of vacuum cleaners Hoover placed a somewhat ambiguous message: men were advised to give their wives a war bond for Christmas but not without adding the slogan: "Give her a Hoover and you give her the best."[75] In 1944, women's emancipation was still far away.

Ads in Life Magazine. General Electric (21 Dec. 1942), Curtiss Wright (20 Dec. 1943), Coca-Cola (18 Dec. 1944) and Whitman's Chocolates (18 Dec. 1944).

Christmas in the White House promised to be modest in 1944. Eleanor Roosevelt had written in her column that she had encountered problems buying decorations for the Christmas tree in the East Room. On December 23 a Girl Scout brought two boxes with homemade Christmas decorations made of peanuts, straws, paper napkins and red ribbons. The First Lady was very pleased and thought the decorated tree "very charming and as Christmas-y as anything I have ever seen."[76] The Roosevelt family celebrated Christmas again at their Springwood Estate in Hyde Park, New York, from where the President also delivered his Christmas address. "Our enemies still fight," he said. "They still have reserves of men and military power. But they themselves know that they and their evil works are doomed."[77] He put military personnel and civilians at ease by saying, "The tide of battle has turned, slowly but inexorably, against those who sought to destroy civilization."[78]

In the freezing cold of Washington, D.C., some 15,000 people had gathered outside the White House to sing Christmas carols and to listen to the speeches. At the First Lady's special request, injured military service people from the Walter Reed Hospital attended. This year again, as in 1942 and 1943, the outdoor Christmas tree was not lighted, but inside the East Room, the bulbs of a Christmas tree glowed. Better times lay ahead for the U.S., but by that time, 1600 Pennsylvania Avenue would have other residents.[79]

Notes chapter II:

[1] Weintraub, S., *15 Stars: Eisenhower, MacArthur, Marshall*, p. 301.
[2] www.historichotelsthenandnow.com/trianonpalaceversailles
[3] Rue, L., 'Censors Reveal Details of Blitz by Gen. S. Claus', *Chicago Tribune*, 26 Dec. 1944.
[4] Kershaw, A. *The Longest Winter: The Epic Story of World War II's Most Decorated Platoon*, p. 149.
[5] 'Allied Services Christmas Celebration Greetings (1944)', British Pathé.
[6] Farris, J., *A Soldier's Sketchbook*, pp. 121-130.
[7] Boston, B. (ed.), *History Of The 398th Infantry Regiment In World War II*, p. 168.
[8] Farris, J., *A Soldier's Sketchbook*, p. 131.
[9] Farris, J., *A Soldier's Sketchbook*, p. 134.
[10] Farris, J., *A Soldier's Sketchbook*, p. 137.
[11] 'Betty Maguson Olson: Letters Home, Christmas, 1944', Minnesota Historical Society's Manuscripts Collection.
[12] Cronkite IV, W. & Isserman, M., *Cronkite's War: His World War II Letters Home*, pp. 267-269.
[13] Weintraub, S, *11 Days in December*, p. 142; Ambrose, S.E., *Citizen Soldiers*, pp. 273-273.
[14] *Kerst aan het front*, EO Tweede Wereldoorlog documentaires, 2005.
[15] *Kerst aan het front*, EO Tweede Wereldoorlog documentaires, 2005.
[16] 'Minn. Church Recalls How Christmas Carols Saved Some U.S. Lives in World War II', *PBS Newshour*, 23 Dec. 2011.
[17] Weintraub, S, *11 Days in December*, p. 142.
[18] Ambrose, S.E., *Citizen Soldiers*, pp. 273-273.
[19] *Kerst aan het front*, EO Tweede Wereldoorlog documentaires, 2005.
[20] 'Minn. Church Recalls How Christmas Carols Saved Some U.S. Lives in World War II', *PBS Newshour*, 23 Dec. 2011.
[21] *Kerst aan het front*, EO Tweede Wereldoorlog documentaires, 2005.
[22] 'Minn. Church Recalls How Christmas Carols Saved Some U.S. Lives in World War II', *PBS Newshour*, 23 Dec. 2011.
[23] Allen, T., 'The Sinking of SS Leopoldville', 14 Apr. 2000, Uboat.net.
[24] Korman, S., 'Chicago Santas give Party for Tiny Alsatians', *Chicago Tribune*, 24 Dec. 1944.
[25] Fisher, R.J., 'A Gift of Oranges', *America in WWII*, Dec. 2010.
[26] Bruyere, A., 'Many Children See First Joyful Yule', *Chicago Tribune*, 25 Dec. 1944.
[27] Beilue, J.M., 'World War II soldier brought American Christmas to French child', *Amarillo Globe-News*, 20 Jul. 206.
[28] 'White Christmas Slows up Action on Front in Italy', *Chicago Tribune*, 26 Dec. 1944.
[29] 'Papal Christmas', *Life Magazine*, 15 Jan. 1945.

[30] 'Pope Opposes Lasting Burden for War Losers', *Chicago Tribune*, 25 Dec. 1944.

[31] Moore, C.P., *Fighting for America*, pp. 266-267.

[32] Black World/Negro Digest, October 1965, p. 11.

[33] Nalty, B., 'The Right to Fight: African-American Marines in World War II', www.nps.gov.

[34] White, W.F., *A Man Called White: The Autobiography of Walter White*, p.280.

[35] Nat Brandt, *Harlem at War: The Black Experience in WWII*, p. 223.

[36] Nalty, B., 'The Right to Fight: African-American Marines in World War II', www.nps.gov.

[37] White, W.F., *A Man Called White: The Autobiography of Walter White*, pp.281-282.

[38] Nalty, B., 'The Right to Fight: African-American Marines in World War II', www.nps.gov; Taylor, J.E., Freedom to Serve: *Truman, Civil Rights, and Executive Order 9981*, pp. 35-36.

[39] Nat Brandt, *Harlem at War: The Black Experience in WWII*, p. 223.

[40] Taylor, J.E., *Freedom to Serve: Truman, Civil Rights, and Executive Order 9981*, pp. 35-36.

[41] Leyva, A., 'Christmas at Hanford', Chemical Heritage Foundation, winter 2008-2009.

[42] Toomey, E., 'The Manhattan Project at Hanford Site', Atomic Heritage Foundation, 01 Mar. 2016.

[43] Kelly, C.C., *Manhattan Project: The Birth of the Atomic Bomb in the Words of Its Creators*, p.223.

[44] Kelly, C.C., *Remembering the Manhattan Project: Perspectives on the Making of the Atomic Bomb and its Legacy*, p. 87.

[45] 'Maj. Glenn Miller, Leader of Air Force Band, Lost in Flight', *Chicago Tribune*, 25 Dec. 1944.

[46] Spragg, D.M., *Glenn Miller Declassified*, p. 287; *Kerst aan het front*, EO Tweede Wereldoorlog documentaires, 2005.

[47] Dietrich, M., *Marlene*, p. 250.

[48] Sassaman, R., 'Hope to the front', *Stars in WWII / America in WWII*, 2010.

[49] Library of Congress, *I'll be Home for Christmas*, p. 58; 'U.S. Merchant Marine in World War II', www.usmm.org/ww2.html.

[50] Hope, B., 'Bob Hope's Christmas 1944 Broadcast to the U.S. Merchant Marine Everywhere', www.usmm.org; 'Maiden Creek: American Steam merchant', Uboat.net.

[51] Hope, B., 'Bob Hope's Christmas 1944 Broadcast to the U.S. Merchant Marine Everywhere', www.usmm.org.

[52] Masuda, H., MacArthur in Asia: The General and His Staff in the Philippines, Japan, and Korea, pp. 164-168.

[53] Weintraub, S., *11 days in December*, pp. 18-19.

[54] 'Million Pounds of Turkey for M'Arthur's Men', *Chicago Tribune*, 24 Dec. 1944.

[55] Zebrowski, C., 'That Chestnut Song', *America in WWII*, Dec. 2010.

[56] Martin, H., 'The Story Behind "Have Yourself A Merry Little Christmas"', website NPR Music, 19 Nov. 2010.

[57] The Library of Congress, *I'll be Home for Christmas*, p. 117.

[58] *A Century of Christmas Memories*, p.57; 'Rationing for the war effort', www.nationalww2museum.org/students-teachers/student-resources/research-starters/take-closer-look-ration-books.

[59] Litt, M., *Christmas 1945*, p.38.

[60] The Library of Congress, *I'll be Home for Christmas*, p. 117.

[61] Weitraub, S., *11 Days in December*, p. 80.

[62] 'Christmas Tree Supply Just Meets the Demand', *Chicago Tribune*, 24 Dec. 1944.

[63] 'Wanted! Christmas wrappings', *Life Magazine*, 25 Dec. 1944.

[64] Felchner, W.J., 'Collectible World War II Christmas Cards', Bukisa.com, 08 Mar. 2010.

[65] Waggoner, S. *Christmas Memories*, pp. 65-66.

[66] Kushian, J., 'Have Yourself a Nasty Little Christmas', *America in WWII*, December 2010; Felchner, W.J., 'Collectible World War II Christmas Cards', Bukisa.com, 08 Mar. 2010.

[67] Thompson, J., *De bevrijding*, p. 31.

[68] *Life Magazine*, 21 Dec. 1942.

[69] *Life Magazine*, 21 Dec. 1942.

[70] *Life Magazine*, 20 Dec. 1943.

[71] *Life Magazine*, 20 Dec. 1943.

[72] *Life Magazine*, 18 Dec. 1944.

[73] *Life Magazine*, 18 Dec. 1944.

[74] *Life Magazine*, 18 Dec. 1944.

[75] *Life Magazine*, 04 Dec. 1944.

[76] Roosevelt, E., *My Day*, 23 Dec. 1944.

[77] 'Prayer for Day of World Peace Voiced by F.D.R.', *Chicago Tribune*, 25 Dec. 1944.

[78] 'History of the National Christmas Tree', NPS.gov.

[79] 'Prayer for Day of World Peace Voiced by F.D.R.', *Chicago Tribune*, 25 Dec. 1944.

- III -
A New and Better World

Although the Blitz, the German bombing offensive on Great Britain, had come to an end in May 1941, fear had returned to the streets of London in 1944. In June of that year, the first German V-1 "flying bomb" (an unmanned missile) had caused many deaths in the British capital. At its climax, over 100 of those flying bombs had been unleashed on the city. In September the even more frightening V-2 rocket had followed, against which the British had hardly any defense because of its speed.[1] According to figures of the British authorities, 6,184 people had been killed in Great Britain by the V-1 and 2,754 by the V-2. Far more people had been injured by them.[2] The majority of these victims fell in the capital, causing some 1 million civilians to flee the city. By using these V-weapons or *Vergeltungswaffen* – weapons of revenge – Hitler hoped he could still win the war, but these attacks achieved little besides sowing fear.

To many Londoners, however, it meant that they would have to spend the Christmas holidays of 1944 for the most part underground once again. Up to 15,000 people, the majority from south London and the north of Kent, had found shelter in the Chislehurst Caves, a system of lime and flint mining galleries in southeast metropolitan London. According to the son of a guard who was on duty there during the war, the shelter was overcrowded at Christmas. The assembled mass of people generated so much warmth that the temperature within the caves was 10°C higher than outside.

During the war, the Chislehurst Caves had been transformed into a veritable subterranean city where people remained for weeks or months on end. Underground were a cinema, a chapel, a civil advisory office and a hospital with a full time staff of a doctor and two nurses. For the use of the sanitary facilities, adults paid a fee of 6 pence a week and children 3. Members of the Women's Voluntary Service, the Red Cross and the Salvation Army provided food that was prepared top side for those in need.[3] During Christmas celebrations underground, concerts and pantomimes were held to entertain, and Salvation Army soldiers sang Christmas carols.[4] Although people had to make do with little in the overcrowded mine passageways and most of those present would have been yearning for a Christmas celebration at home, at least they were safe from the deadly weapons Nazi Germany unleashed on England. While things remained calm on Christmas Day, on Boxing Day a V-2 explosion on MacKenzie Road in the London suburb of Islington claimed 73 deaths in the Prince of Wales pub.[5] The residents of London would have to endure the attacks of V-2s until March 1945 before this terror came to an end.

Because the V-1 and V-2 operated on mechanical automatic guidance systems which did not require light on the ground for identification, and because the piloted bombers of the severely weakened *Luftwaffe* no longer posed a threat, the full blackout had been changed in September to a dim-out. Nevertheless, the light frost and fog during the Christmas holidays heightened the somber mood caused by the recent failure of Operation Market Garden, the attacks by the V-1 and V-2 and the unexpected offensive in the Ardennes. All hopes that the war would be over before the end of the year, had evaporated.[6]

Rationing still had a huge impact on daily life, although the Ministry of Food managed to provide some additional sugar, margarine and meat for everyone. In addition there were sweets for the kids and a small amount of tea for people over the age of 70. Nonetheless, a traditional Christmas dinner with turkey was something most British could only dream of. Still, housewives received well-meant tips for alternative dishes. *Woman's Magazine* for instance, suggested that year to simulate roast turkey with pork filled with apple sauce and bread.[7]

It was more difficult than during the earlier years of the war to obtain alcoholic beverages, in part because a large portion of the production of beer was destined for the military. Instead of grain, other ingredients such as potatoes were increasingly used for beer. As the army requisitioned most of the wood as well, the brew was stored in clay pots instead of wooden casks.[8] A positive side effect of the shortage of alcohol was that far fewer people needed to be arrested for being drunk and disorderly.[9]

In 1944 in the U.K., Christmas presents were extremely hard to come by. However, Mavis Kimberley, from the city of Lincoln, recalls she was not disappointed this year: "I had been given 4 books, some hankies, a padded coat hanger, a pen and a face flannel," she remembered after the war. "What would today's children think of these gifts?" Christmas decorations were scarcely for sale either. According to Mavis, all of their Christmas decorations got so "tatty" after years of use that there was hardly any green left on the artificial tree and nearly all Christmas balls had broken. Since it was impossible to buy something new, the family made their own chains from strips of aluminum foil her brother had brought home one day. Bundles of them had fallen from a truck on the way to one of the air bases in the area.

It was only after the war that Mavis and her family understood what those strips were used for. The British called these strips of foil "chaff" or "window," and they were dropped out of aircraft in large quantities to blind German radar.[10] Other families used the strips as an alternative for Christmas decorations as well. In Berchtesgaden in Germany for instance, Irmgard A. Hunt-Paul and her sister had decorated a young fir tree from the forest with a supply of "strips of silver paper" they had collected "that just came falling from the sky after enemy aircraft had passed overhead."[11]

Just as in the United States, in Great Britain the volume of Christmas mail was massive: the Royal Mail counted 350 million postal items.[12] Many British again this year sought solace in the churches. During this sixth wartime Christmas, the archbishop of York inspired his fellow believers with courage. "The danger of invasion has passed," he declared "and the worst of the air raids are over. With quiet confidence we see the end in sight. ... And though we know that there will be a hard struggle both in Europe and in the Far East before victory is won, we begin to plan and to look forward to a new and better world."[13]

In his last Christmas address of the war, King George voiced his wish for a "world of free men untouched by tyranny."[14] Those were sweet words but the British had had to listen to them for years. Most important for many of them was the fact that they and their next of kin were still alive. Joan Styan from London for instance had a brush with death when a V-2 rocket came down very close to her. One of her cousins serving in the navy was reported missing and had probably drowned. She stated how she and the other family members "despite all the fear, together with these sad things that had happened, we saw yet another Christmas and were lucky to be safe and sound and all together especially as my father managed to get home on leave from the Navy. Everyone's hopes and dreams were relying on the New Year when we were desperately hoping that it would bring peace and freedom."[15]

British military in western Europe made only a minor contribution to the Ardennes offensive. They were recuperating from Operation Market Garden and the battle for Walcheren and were preparing to advance into Germany the next year. Soldier Tom Hilton had an exhausting and anxious time under his belt after he had settled down in Nijmegen on Christmas in the liberated southern part of the Netherlands. A member of the Royal Army Ordnance Corps, responsible for repairs and supply, he had landed on Sword Beach in Normandy on D-Day +1, driving a Bren Gun Carrier, a light, armored tracked vehicle. While driving the vehicle through the surf in the direction of the beach, he had been terrified. He said that he kept his eyes shut so he did not have to see anything of the battlefield around him. During the ensuing campaign in Normandy he drove a truck for weeks on end, by night and by day, delivering supplies to the front, without lights and in an unknown area without sign posts. It happened frequently that convoys got lost, were subjected to enemy fire or hit a land mine. He was very lucky himself, but one night he lost two of his mates who were driving in the trucks in front of and behind him and were killed by land mines. After the war it would trouble him deeply that he had survived and they had not.

Tom Hilton ended up in the Netherlands by way of France and Belgium, and prior to the Christmas holidays he was billeted in the home of a Dutch family with two children. As the family had nothing in the house to celebrate Christmas with, Hilton and his mates put aside some of their chocolate rations to give to the children as a present. After the war, Hilton admitted he cried on Christmas morning when he saw the pure joy on the faces of the children being presented with a small bar of chocolate. It was the only time during the war he had cried, despite all the violent events he had experienced. He donated his ration of cigarettes to the parents. They were so grateful, they gave him their camera as a present when he left Nijmegen. He really thought he could not accept it, but the grateful Dutch told him it was of no use to them any more as they could not buy new rolls of film. After having accepted the present, Hilton and his unit advanced towards Germany. After crossing the Rhine he served as a motorcycle dispatch rider, and he drove supply trucks until the end of the war. The camera would be used after the war by his son, who took pictures of railway engines with it in his youth. He was careful with it as he knew it had a special meaning to his father.[16]

A little less than 43 miles south of Nijmegen, British lieutenant Keith R. Thresher and his artillery regiment celebrated Christmas with the locals of Maasbree in the Dutch province of Limburg. The British had invited the villagers to join them on Christmas Eve for dinner in their camp and to participate in the party afterwards. Some soldiers had prepared small acts. One of them took his role as the bad guy so seriously that he, according to Thresher, "could be seen at all hours of the day and night enacting, with the aid of a mirror, vicious Nazi-like facial expressions." Another British soldier had borrowed a piano "for the small sum of two tins of bully, 10 cigarettes, a tube of toothpaste and a smile." He had also persuaded a woman to sing at the party. After having lived for a month on mainly corned beef, the Christmas dinner of canned turkey, pork, beer, rum and Christmas pudding was something the men had been looking forward to for a long time. To the Dutch, it must have been a veritable feast as, according to Thresher, they "ate as though they had not eaten for years." After dinner, the party went into high gear. Many British were "bowled over like ninepins" after having drunk punch, and a Dutchman who had been drinking too much even had to be taken home on a stretcher that day. Some British party goers placed bets on who would catch a swaying mate when he fell over. Another soldier collapsed with emotion when listening to the Dutch woman singing "Ave Maria."[17] It looked as though all stress and tension of the past months were being partied away that Christmas Day.

Such wild parties meant nothing to Sergeant Len Scott of the Royal Army Pay Corps in Rome. In his opinion, December 25th was "a sparkling day with the distant mountains sharp against a deep blue sky." He and his comrade, Staff-Sergeant Gordon Milne, decided together to skip the "boozy Mess Christmas dinner" with their colleagues and go to town instead. They had "an excellent Christmas dinner" on the Via Nazionale near the fire of an open hearth in an art gallery where all the paintings had been taken down from the walls. While an Italian artist was busily painting a landscape on the wall, it did not take Scott much trouble to imagine how Renaissance painters like Domenico Ghirlandaio or Benozzo Gozzoli had been working there 500 years ago. Although Scott and Milne were both almost total abstainers, they toasted each other's health and "a quick return home." When dinner was done, they relaxed for a few hours on large sofas in the lounge and then attended an opera performance. The next morning, they were reprimanded by their sergeant major for their absence at the Christmas dinner. Scott and his mate defended themselves by saying there was no rule whatsoever that made their presence mandatory. Their superior who according to Scott, had not yet recovered from the drinking orgy of the day before, called us "a pair of 'unsociable misfits' and dismissed us contemptuously."

Sergeant Scott was not sorry at all for having missed Christmas dinner. The climax had been "a drunkenly-aggressive N.C.O. who was hung by his ankles over the stair-well 'to cool him off'. There was a tally of smashed glasses and broken bottles for which the Mess fund would have to account." A few days later he and Milne had an experience during an excursion in Rome that well made up for the collision with their superior. A member of the Swiss Guard invited them to their mess in Vatican City. "We were welcomed by a dozen of his mates," Scott described after the war "and, after much good food and wine, were invited to exchange our battle-dress for the Guards' ceremonial uniform. Behold us then – an Englishman and a Scotsman kitted out with baggy trousers, steel breast-plates and Conquistador-style steel helmets. Add two halberds and we were dressed to kill!"[18] With this experience and all impressions he had gathered in Algeria and Italy since his departure from Great Britain in 1942, he returned home in December 1945, just in time to celebrate Christmas in his home in Surrey with his wife Minna from whom he had been apart for five years.[19]

Ivor Walter Chappell, who had spent the previous Christmas in a lonely port, served during the 1944 Christmas period on a ship in the middle of the Atlantic Ocean as part of a convoy of 30 vessels bound for the U.S. The sailor found it "a lovely place to be" although he described the storm that had lasted for three days in the period prior to Christmas as "a very frightening experience. The ship pitched and tossed and you literally took your life in your hands to go up top deck!" The fact that the ship's hold was empty only added to the misery caused by the waves. No one aboard bothered about Christmas approaching, because according to Chappell they lived from one day to the next without ever looking at a calendar. When the time eventually came, they could not ignore any longer that Christmas had arrived. "You'll never see anything like this ever again," someone called from up top and everyone scrambled up the ladder to the deck. There they were surprised by a spectacular view of an American destroyer which had joined the convoy. According to Chappell "this wasn't just any old destroyer, it was garlanded in pretty decorations, all up the masts, all around the bridge, signs saying 'A Merry Christmas'. The best bit was, and I'll never forget it, Father Christmas in full regalia standing proud, up on the bridge on a raised platform, waving his beard at us and shouting through a megaphone: 'Ho, ho, ho, a Merry Christmas everyone!'" Sturdy seamen were moved to tears on hearing the choir singing "Silent Night" aboard the American vessel. The Christmas atmosphere remained until Chappell's vessel berthed in New Jersey where the snow was thick on the ground and the temperature below zero.[20]

Notes chapter III:

[1] Holmes, R., *40-45: van Blitzkrieg tot Hiroshima*, pp. 278-279.
[2] Risbey, P.N., 'Air Raid Precautions - Deaths and injuries 1939-45', 2002.
[3] *Wartime Farm Christmas* Special, BBC, 2012.
[4] Brown, M., *A Wartime Christmas*, p. 9.
[5] *Wartime Farm Christmas* Special, BBC, 2012;
www.warmemorialsonline.org.uk/memorial/253877.
[6] Brown, M., *Christmas on the Home Front*, p. 164.
[7] Brown, M., *A Wartime Christmas*, p. 12.
[8] *Wartime Farm Christmas* Special, BBC, 2012.
[9] Brown, M., *Christmas on the Home Front*, p. 75.
[10] Kimberley, M., 'Christmas time', *BBC WW2 People's War*, 26 Jul. 2005.
[11] Hunt, I.A., *Op schoot bij Hitler*, p. 195.
[12] Brown, M., *Christmas on the Home Front*, p. 175.
[13] Brown, M., *Christmas on the Home Front*, p. 164.
[14] Brown, M., *Christmas on the Home Front*, p. 181.
[15] Styan, J, 'Entertainments and a Wartime Christmas: In London', *BBC WW2 People's War*, 17 Jun. 2004.
[16] Hilton, J., 'The Wartime Stories Of Tom Hilton, My Grandad', *BBC WW2 People's War*, 05 Mai 2004.
[17] Thresher, K., 'Christmas Day on the Front Line (Taken from F for Fox)', *BBC WW2 People's War*, 09 Nov. 2004.
[18] Scott, L., 'Contrasts: Christmas in Rome and in England, 1944', *BBC WW2 People's War*, 28 Mar. 2005.
[19] Scott, L., 'Home Again: Warlingham, Surrey. 1945-47', *BBC WW2 People's War*, 10 Mai 2005.
[20] Chappell, I.W., 'Some Christmas's Remembered - 1942, 43, 44 and 45', *BBC WW2 People's War*, 17 Apr. 2005.

- IV -
Kriegsweihnacht

On Christmas Eve in a ward in a German hospital, an *Oberleutnant* lay motionless in bed. It was warm and quiet in the room where he was being treated for the severe injuries he had sustained on the Murmansk front. As he lay there in the corner near the stove, his head on a white pillow, it looked as if he were already dead. His eyes in a pale face were shut, and life seemed to be slipping away from him. All of a sudden, the door of the room was carefully opened and the dark room was lit by the cheerfully shimmering candles in a small fir tree. The soft sounds of German Christmas carols sung by children came closer and closer. As if by miracle, the eyes of the injured soldier opened. Laboriously, he raised himself to see where the light and the singing were coming from. While staring at the lights in the tree, his thoughts went back to past Christmas Days at home. A little smile appeared on his face. "He wants to live," so the story continues, "to live for the *Heimat* (fatherland) so far away but never so close as in this fateful moment, by the light of the Christmas tree. ... And he feels joyous and happy: in this holy moment his fate returns from the frontier of death to within range of life itself. He will be cured."[1]

This story about a miraculous healing by the light of a Christmas tree was published in 1944 in the propaganda bulletin *"Deutsche Kriegsweihnacht"* (German War Christmas). Starting in 1941, each year prior to the Christmas holidays, the department of culture of the propaganda office of the NSDAP (National Socialist German Workers' Party) issued a compilation of Christmas stories for adults and children, this one being the last. The 1944 issue contained Christmas stories from the front during World War I, such as one about a soldier in France who, while on patrol close to enemy lines, risked his life while fetching a Christmas tree in order to celebrate Christmas. Furthermore, it contained letters to and from the front, poems and folk songs, all of course along the lines of the Nazi Christmas celebration. For the children, it contained fairy tales of Snow White and Mother Holle by the Grimm brothers.

*A German soldier risks his life taking a Christmas tree to his own lines.
Image from "Deutsche Kriegsweihnacht" of 1944. (Author's collection)*

Speeches by the master of propaganda, Joseph Goebbels, could not be left out of course. A posthumously published contribution of an ode to the German Christmas celebration was included: National Socialist writer and poet Kurt Eggers died in 1943 at the Eastern front serving with the *Waffen-SS*. He argued Christmas was not about "giving love" and "legends from the far away Jewish land" but about "freedom, honor and justice." He described the Christmas tree as the symbol of the "grandeur of the struggling and defiant life that in danger and in need holds out against any fearsome and difficult situation." According to him, Christmas became "the celebration of victory and the required willingness to fight. ... We therefore do not celebrate our *Weihnachtsfest* in the sentimental mood, contained in so many strange Christmas carols, but in the hard and inflexible knowledge that we, as the perennial torch bearers, are destined to carry the light of freedom in the world."[2]

Despite Eggers' jubilant words, the tone of the Nazi Christmas book was gloomier than before, as the circumstances at the fronts did not justify any festivities. Yearning for the *Heimat* had become a more important theme than the victories and the expansion of the Third Reich. This was for instance the case in the story about a *Volksdeutsche* (someone of German ancestry living outside the German borders) farmer who was traveling by horse-drawn cart from Russia in wintry conditions with his wife, children and grandfather in order to settle in Germany. The return to Germany of people of German ancestry was an idea the Nazis propagated with the slogan *"Heim ins Reich"* (Back home to the Reich). In the story, the farmer's wife was pregnant with their fifth child and the old man hoped to reach German soil so he could die there. Straw and blankets in the cart protected the passengers from the cold.

On Christmas Eve they had reached a forest on the farthest frontier of the Reich where, in the winter night, their child was born. Women from other families, who were traveling with them to the Reich, had lighted a fire in the forest and had prepared something warm for the mother. "It was a miracle," they said. "Entirely healthy and well built, it had come into this world in the middle of the eastern winter. Yes, yes, the sturdy farmers' blood." The child was swaddled and laid down in the cart between the blankets. "And as the wind softly stroked the tree tops," the story continues, "it was as if they sang a lullaby for the baby."

Suddenly the woman saw her child "look out with its eyes wide open. Then the mother saw it too: a miracle had happened. A bright light radiated from the fir tree standing high and tall in the night sky. A light like stardust lay over all its branches! Tall and festive, the shining tree stood in the winter night and it was more beautiful to see than all Christmas trees in the world." The next morning, people from the other carts came to look at the child who had been born during the "great exodus." The writer's source of inspiration needs no further explanation. "The first child had been born in the *Heimat* – now new life began for all."[3]

In another Nazi publication, the bulletin *"Die Neue Gemeinschaft"* (The New Society) issued by the department of ceremonies and holidays of the NSDAP, a speech had been printed prior to the holidays that party leaders could deliver at Christmas to the injured in military hospitals. It was written by Nazi author and poet Thilo Scheller who had found inspiration in a poem by 19th century poet Wilhelm Weber, *"Es wächst viel Brot in der Winternacht"* (Much grain grows during winter's night), which was the title of the speech as well. The message of the poem was that beneath the snow of winter, seeds for grain lie dormant in expectation of spring, a prediction it was hoped, would be applicable to the Third Reich as well. The speech also stated: "Even the most hard-boiled soldier, the most dashing dare-devil, is not embarrassed to turn soft for an evening – when it is Christmas in Germany, and wherever there are Germans."

Christmas brought back memories of old Christmas carols, of the lights in the Christmas tree and of mothers and girlfriends. Injured or sick soldiers should be told that their hearts were allowed to be home, but they should not be homesick. The people's community "that our Führer Adolf Hitler has given us, will not forget those who cannot celebrate Christmas with their loved ones." They should derive hope from the presence of the nurses, whose names like Inge or Gertrud would feel dependable. Christmas was not to be celebrated too exuberantly at a time "when all the strengths of the front and homeland are needed for the war effort, when our comrades in the field are surrounded by filth and hardly know where to find a small tree and a miserable Christmas candle."

"The enemy has laid in ruins many treasured buildings, many quiet corners, many familiar dwellings where shining Christmas trees stood year after year," the speech continued. "Yet he cannot destroy those fir trees in the forest, rooted in German earth, nor can he destroy our hearts that are even more firmly rooted in the German people. Even in the ruins of cities destroyed by Negro pilots who have not the faintest inkling of what a German Christmas means." Here, reference is made to the attempt of July 20th that year when "providence preserved the Führer because it needs him for the future of our people, also so that our children will be able to celebrate Christmas in peace and joy." The guests to be invited were "all our dead comrades from all the battlefields of Europe. ... They should be with us in spirit, not as pale ghosts, but in the fullness of their youth. That should teach us that the morale in the homeland is worthy of our soldiers at the front!"

The text ended as follows: "My dear comrades, war has been called the father of all things, but it also gives depth and meaning to the most motherly of all festivals, one that gives our people the strength to end this war with victory, to banish everything superficial and false and foreign. The grain will grow in stillness from the depths, producing the bread that we, God grant, will eat in peace."[4]

With the publication of *"Deutsche Kriegsweihnacht"* and the mandatory speech to injured and sick soldiers, the Nazi regime showed in 1944 that it still wanted to exert influence on the way the Germans celebrated Christmas, as it had in the 1930s. In order not to endanger the relationship with Christians during the war, the Christian Christmas celebration was not directly attacked. Hence in the *Wehrmacht*, chaplains were not prevented from conducting religious Christmas celebrations. Attempts were still being made, though, to introduce new Christmas practices that matched the Nazi world view. An increasingly important emphasis was placed at Christmastime on reverence for the soldiers who had died for the Fatherland, as had been the case during the previous world war. It was an attempt to lend a positive sense to the grieving of many German families over the loss of a father, husband or son.

Around Christmas a cult of death was promoted with stories, songs, poems and drawings. The Nazi Christmas book of 1944, for instance, showed a drawing of an illuminated Christmas tree surrounded by soldiers' graves marked by Iron Crosses.[5] A much published expression of this reverence for death was the poem *"Der toten Soldaten Heimkehr"* (the return of the dead soldiers) by Thilo Schiller. "And when the candles burn down on the tree of light", one of the lines read, "the dead soldier places his earth-encrusted hand lightly on each of the children's young heads. We died for you, for we believed in Germany."[6] The "Ghosts of Christmas Past, Present and Yet to Come" were amateurs in comparison to this Christmas horror. The poet also thought of phrases the children had to recite on

Christmas when lighting the candles of an Advent wreath one by one and respectively naming the mother, the poor, the dead and the *Führer*.[7]

Christmas tree on German war graves.
Image from "Deutsche Kriegsweihnacht" of 1944. (Author's collection)

Nazi propaganda makers encouraged mothers and widows to decorate a picture of their son or husband, fallen at the front, with a fir branch, to lay a place at table for him during the Christmas dinner and to light a red candle in the Christmas tree for him. They also wanted to relocate part of the Christmas celebration to cemeteries of fallen soldiers and war memorial sites. Placing candles or even small Christmas trees on graves was encouraged although it must be noted here that lighting candles on graves was a tradition that existed before 1933 so this was no invention of the Nazis at all. How many Germans followed these instructions is hard to determine, although the shortage of candles surely did not help one bit.[8]

For those on the German home front, the shortage of candles was the least of their worries in 1944. Apart from the depressing fear or grief over the fate of family members and friends at the front, Allied bombing raids and shortages of almost everything made celebrating Christmas the traditional way all but impossible. The shortage of food had become serious. In those parts of Germany already occupied by the Allies, potatoes and bread constituted the main food, according to American correspondent Larry Rue. In addition, civilians were given a little over seven ounces of meat once a week. Children were begging American soldiers for candy, chewing gum and chocolate, as they did elsewhere in Europe.[9] In the part of Germany still under Nazi rule, the government attempted to raise spirits by increasing the Christmas rations with 1 gram of butter and coffee, ¼ liter of schnapps (German liquor) and 10 cigarettes.

On bulletin boards, this *Sonderzuteiling* (special distribution) was presented as a favor of the *Führer*. The Nazi newspaper *Der Völkische Beobachter* published tips on how to put together a nutritious and varied Christmas dinner, despite the shortages. The entrée was soup made of dried vegetables; the main dish could be a choice between cabbage rolls stuffed with barley, white cabbage in flour sauce or fried cabbage with onions. Dessert consisted of artificial cream made from skimmed milk and flour.[10]

Sauerkraut and potatoes were the items on the Christmas menu of Herbert R. Vogt in Berlin. He had become a *Flakhelfer* (helper in anti-aircraft defense) and was put to work fighting fires during air raids. Traveling to the Tegel suburb prior to Christmas he had already sensed a defeatist atmosphere. "Wherever you went, there was a pervasive atmosphere in the air of impending downfall in personal lives as much as in the nation's existence," he wrote. In the train, littered with filth and trash, he had seen how his fellow passengers could not be bothered by slogans like "Down with Hitler and Long Live Stalin" written on the walls in red paint. "I could sense it that most Berliners already knew, by a strange gut feeling, that this was their last Christmas before Germany's doomsday. Any way you looked at it, there was very little to celebrate and to celebrate with. Ultra-short rations, constant stress, and much of the Capital being reduced to rubble in never-ending air raids were not putting people in the mood for the upcoming holidays. The theme of Christmas is peace on earth, and when you are about to face death, then this noble message is nothing but a joke."[11]

At Christmas he was on leave, and he returned to Tegel on December 22 – feeling dejected about the desperate state in Germany – in order to spend the Christmas holidays with his mother and grandmother. Their warm welcome and the fact they were still alive, cheered him up. It was so cold in the apartment, though, that the next morning he set about collecting a great load of wood in the forest to heat the apartment. He transported it on his sledge on which he also took a "petite but neat and trim-looking pine tree, begging me to take it home." Back home, his mother immediately started decorating the tree while his grandmother did the cooking. She had a small job for her grandson as well and gave him "a long knife with a six-inch blade" to kill the rabbit because she wanted to make rabbit stew. Herbert refused. When his grandmother said that as a soldier he had been trained to shoot people, he answered: "That is a bad analogy. We are shooting the enemy to protect you from getting killed by the bombs they dump on us. Why should I kill the poor little animal when it has not done me any harm?" Eventually, the animal lover was willing to hold the animal upside down enabling his grandmother to cut its throat. His mother collected the blood in a bowl to make a sauce with it, adding onions, chunks of bacon and herbs, while his grandmother skinned the rabbit – a skill which she had learned as a girl on the farm. "Christmas Eve in my mother's place turned out better than I expected," Vogt continued. "We did not exchange any gifts; the big-tiled stove kept the living room warm, and the best of all, we didn't have to go to bed hungry." He refused to take even a small bite of the rabbit meat, but he satisfied himself with the potatoes and the sauerkraut. The Christmas tree and a letter from his father at the front in Hungary made the celebration complete.[12]

In his home in Berlin there was no Christmas tree for Wolfgang Pickert, then 15 years of age. According to him, this tradition was forbidden because of the fire hazard.[13] Whether such an order did actually exist or not is unknown but it seems logical enough. Each time Berliners rushed to the air raid shelter when the alarm sounded, there was, of course, no time to extinguish the candles in the tree. If a house was missed by the bombs, it really would have been very unfortunate if it burned down due to a lighted Christmas tree. During the Christmas holidays, Berliners spent much time in underground shelters although it remained quiet.[14]

In Munich as well, the Christmas spirit was dampened by the fear of Allied bombardments. After Wolfhilde von König had finished writing Christmas letters to all her friends on December 17, she was pulled out of her Christmas mood by the air raid alarm that night at 22:00. For the third time that day, she and her mother rushed to the cellar. "We had barely gotten down below when it started," she wrote in her diary the next day. "It was really awful; it had never been this bad before. A bomb must have come down very close by. Finally this hell stopped and we could go outside to check on the conditions. How it looked there! The buildings at Steindorfstrasse numbers five, six and seven had simply disappeared. The corner house, number eight, was completely engulfed in flames. Our apartment was in total chaos; no doors or window anymore, walls crumbled, ceilings fallen down. It was a sad picture of destruction. There wasn't much we could do." The bombardment by the British that night claimed 562 dead.[15]

The next morning she and her mother were in the home for the homeless to help distribute food and other necessities to bombed-out fellow citizens. They made their own apartment habitable again and blacked out the windows once more. Despite everything, they did celebrate Christmas on December 24. In the morning they rigged a small Christmas tree and had their Christmas dinner in the home for the homeless. "Dinner was a cold meal," Wolfhilde noted in her diary, "and everyone was surprised at the large portions. We all really liked it. Also, the tables were very nicely decorated. Apples, pine branches and candles on white paper gave a very festive impression. Under the watchful eye of the attending children, the candles in the large Christmas tree were lit. Everyone was enchanted by the sight of the lighted tree, which for us Germans is a symbol and sign of reappearing light."

After everything in the center had been cleared, Wolfhilde and her mother returned to their home where they remembered their father and brother Manny by the light of six candles in their own tree.[16] Emanuel had been serving in the military since the summer of 1943, initially as *Flakhelfer* and subsequently in the *Reichsarbeitsdienst* (State labor service) in the Sudetenland. Towards Christmas 1944, he had been drafted into the *Kriegsmarine* (German navy) and served on the heavy cruiser *Lützow* after training in Flensburg. In the spring of 1945, he would take part in the fighting against the Red Army in the streets of Berlin. He was made a prisoner of war by the Soviets and was released in June 1946. Wolfhilde's and Manny's father came home in June 1945. Wolfhilde also survived the war and passed away in 1993; her brother died in 2009.[17]

In Berchtesgaden, too, the war could no longer be ignored in 1944. Although Hitler's Berghof on the Obersalzberg would be destroyed by bombs in 1945, precautionary measures had been taken by order of Hitler as early as 1943. Anti-aircraft batteries were established on the Kehlstein, the mountain top on which Hitler's tea house stood, and a chemical system was installed in order to shroud the Berghof and other possible targets in artificial fog. Hitler's chalet was camouflaged and a subterranean bunker was built that was opened on Christmas Eve 1943.[18]

In the village of Berchtesgaden itself, it had become more difficult to obtain food. Therefore, Irmgard Paul was very fortunate with her own kitchen garden and her chicken's eggs which provided a welcome addition to their rations. That year, she had voluntarily joined the *Jungmädel* (Nazi association for young girls) but towards the Christmas holidays, she said, her enthusiasm for it had decreased. Although her mother still had a waxen image of Hitler hanging on the wall of her living room, she too had lost her faith in a happy ending to the war. She still had her fighting spirit, but she had also said she had wanted Hitler to be killed on July 20th so that the war would be over sooner.

As the conditions in the Alpine village were still far better than in other German cities, the family had temporarily taken in a boy in connection with the *Kinderlandverschickung* (a Nazi project to evacuate children to safer areas). Other families in the village had also taken in evacuated children. Another reminder of war was the air raid warning that sounded from time to time, causing Irmgard, her sister and mother to seek shelter in their potato cellar. As her mother was unable to buy Christmas presents that year, she gave the girls "two books about nature from Daddy's bookshelf." Christmas dinner consisted of dumplings, sauerkraut and a piece of meat.

On Christmas Eve, in the open air as usual, they commemorated their father who had died at the front three years before. "I could no longer remember what he looked like without looking at photographs," Irmgard wrote in her memoirs. "The man himself was slowly fading into the past, and yet I still missed him." Her mother wrote in her diary that, despite everything, it still was a "*gemütliche Weihnachten*" (cozy Christmas) although they felt very dejected "about what was to come." The three of them would survive. Irmgard emigrated to the United States after the war where she married and had two children.[19]

In 1944, the head of the SS, Heinrich Himmler, celebrated Christmas for the first time without his wife and Poppie, as he called his daughter Gudrun. Undoubtedly, the *Reichsführer-SS* was far too busy with the new tasks, allotted to him by Hitler. Although lacking any military experience whatsoever, in September he had been put in command of the *Volkssturm*, a militia consisting of men between the ages of 16 and 60 ineligible for regular military service. Armed with weapons from World War I, *Panzerfäuste* (anti-tank weapons) and whatever kind of simple weapons they could lay their hands on, these predominantly very young or very old men were to establish a last line of defense against the advancing enemy. In addition, in November Himmler was appointed Commander-in-Chief of *Heeresgruppe Oberrhein*, an army group that was to halt the Allied advance from France.[20] He was no good at all at it. "The responsibility weighs heavily," he wrote in a Christmas letter to his wife, "considering the life of so many Germans depends on whatever I order here, and whose wives and mothers will then have to mourn them, and in a larger sense the lives of 90 million of our people also depend on it." Despite a lack of time and opportunity, he had sent some presents to his "darling Mummy," like a silver plate, a blue handbag, underwear and stockings, and for his daughter a gold bracelet, a sports dress and other things. More was to follow, like a case of mathematical instruments and an old book on botany. He ended his letter as follows: "I wish you, my best Mummy, all the love for Christmas and I hope you'll be at least a little glad with my presents. Many greetings and kisses. Your Daddy."[21]

While on the western front the fighting raged on during the Christmas holidays, it was quiet, generally speaking, in the northern part of the eastern front after the Russians had made huge territorial gains over the past summer. The border of the former Germany in eastern Prussia had been crossed by the Soviets, but the advance in the direction of Berlin would continue in the new year. The Red Army still had a hard time holding the line, though. Some of the farmers who had fled before the feared enemy earlier on, had even returned to their farms recaptured by the *Wehrmacht*. The relatively peaceful Christmas in eastern Prussia had evoked memories of earlier days. The Germans celebrated their last Christmas in this area.

"It was quiet at the front," writer Arno Surminski, raised in eastern Prussia recalls, "and it was quiet in the countryside. A second layer of snow fell on the first. And then one more Christmas. It was just like before all over again: home-made biscuits, fried meat of freshly slaughtered pigs and the usual Christmas rations of tobacco and schnapps."

In Königsberg, today Kaliningrad in Russia, eight-year-old Ingetraud Lippmann was baking cookies of marmalade and four types of fruit for Christmas together with her mother and brother. Her mother had started collecting the ingredients weeks before. While outside it was cold and snowing, the aroma of baking "drifted through the entire house, and the crumbs or the stolen cookies, still warm, tasted so good that waiting for Christmas seemed far too long for us." On Christmas Day, her grandparents and her mother's sister paid them a visit. They had trouble getting there by tram as the rails had been damaged during the bombing.

That afternoon, the family attended a service in the Herzog-Albrecht-Gedächtniskirche – opened in 1913. They went there, walking through the deep snow and heard the church bells ring. "The priest prayed for peace with us," so Lippmann recalls. "I saw many adults wiping tears from their eyes." Back home, the Christmas gifts were distributed. Just like very year, Ingetraud was given "freshly made clothes" for her doll, and for her brother "a hand-made new wooden car lay under the Christmas tree." Finally they could eat their cookies. Although they enjoyed the light and the scent of the burning candles in the fir tree and the candles on the table with gifts, this Christmas was different from others. Prior to the handing out of presents, no Christmas carols were sung, and instead of "sleigh rides and the celebration," the only conversation was about the imminent escape.[22]

For other families in eastern Prussia, Christmas was far from trouble-free either because the Red Army was deeply feared. In Nazi propaganda, much attention had been given to the blood bath Soviet soldiers had created on October 21st, 1944, among the inhabitants of Nemmersdorf in the far eastern part of Prussia. Ella Brümmer, the owner of an eastern Prussian estate, recalled that on Christmas Eve, many people took a walk through the forest and fields to overcome their fear. During the Christmas celebration with wine and treats, the fact that this undoubtedly was their last Christmas in this part of Germany was not spoken about, as it would indeed disappear behind the Iron Curtain after the war.[23]

For those Germans from the east who had fled from the enemy earlier on, the conditions for celebrating Christmas were usually somber. Rosemarie Arndt-Grusdas, at the time 16 years old, and her mother had fled their farm in former Schwirbeln in the Insterburg district. She had enjoyed a protected and carefree youth on the farm where they kept cows, chickens and pigs and grew vegetables and grain. It had been intended that everything would be inherited by her brother, who had been injured at the front and had been admitted to a hospital near Berlin to have his arm amputated.

While mother and daughter traveled westwards in a carriage drawn by two horses, father stayed behind to defend Schwirbeln against the Red Army and to harvest the remaining grain. The roads the women traveled on were congested with other refugees. They had taken their bed covers to keep warm and food for themselves and the horses. En route, they slept in schools, gyms and even sometimes on farms. They weren't hungry yet: once in a while they were even offered warm drinks and soup. "But we were afraid," Rosemarie admitted after the war, "very much so." Their journey of some 124 miles ended in Winkenhagen, Mohrungen District, and still in eastern Prussia. Two days before Christmas her father arrived with a small Christmas tree but without presents.

It was a cheerless Christmas, without her brother and surrounded by strange people who were not overly happy with the refugees. They were uncertain about what was in store for them although Rosemarie's mother fostered hopes of returning home in spring. A few cookies were the only things they ate now. Rosemarie recalled past Christmases which had always been the highlight of the year for her as a child. "Then, pigs, geese and ducks were slaughtered, fir branches collected from the woods and hung over the fireplace," she recalled, "and cookies were baked and a Christmas parcel from the next of kin in Berlin. All this seemed to be over suddenly. There was worse to come however." In mid-January, troops of the Red Army entered Winkenhagen where mother and daughter were still staying. As Soviet tanks trundled into the village and fierce "shooting was going on," Rosemarie and her mother hid beneath their carriage. "Ahead of us, I saw a mother and her young child fall in front of the carriage, shot. And I thought: now the end has come."

It hadn't, not yet anyway, but a lot of suffering still awaited her. Along with other boys and girls, the next day Rosemarie was taken to an out-of-the-way house where she and the girls were raped by Soviet soldiers. Towards the end of January, she was deported with other women to the east where she was put to work in several settings, including in a limestone quarry and on a fruit plantation. Many fellow sufferers perished during their imprisonment. It was only in October 1948 that Rosemarie returned to Germany where she was reunited with her family in Berlin.[24]

Despite the prospects at the front being less than hopeful for the Germans, Christmas celebrations were still held for the military. To *Gefreiter* Joseph Wirth, born in 1926, it was a Germanic celebration such as the Nazis liked. The youngster had been drafted in 1943, along with the other boys of his class of the Gymnasium in Würzburg. In September 1944, he underwent training at the school for N.C.O.s of the armored forces in Potsdam-Nedlitz. As a location for the Christmas celebration, an abandoned stone or sand quarry was selected. When darkness fell, Joseph and his fellow trainees, marched in their dress uniforms to the location, still unknown to them. "This was marked and surrounded by flaming torches," he recalled after the war. "Scattered across the terrain and lighted by fire were rune signs made of birch wood. A Germanic initiation scene like in a picture book!" Battle songs about the victory were sung, stirring speeches were given and poems recited. As "crowning finale", the Nazi Christmas carol "Hohe Nacht der klaren Sterne" (holy night of the clear stars) was sung instead of "Silent Night".

From beginning to end, the entire meeting was in line with the directives of the party concerning Christmas celebrations. Apparently, the program had not been received well by all: in the officers' barracks, Wirth noted that the officers had not liked it.[25] It must have been a surrealistic scene: as the Third Reich was about to collapse, Christmas was celebrated as if a German victory were within reach.

At the front, Christmas celebrations were less bombastic. In Kurland in Latvia, Swedish Erik Wallin and his mates of the *11. SS-Freiwilligen-Panzergrenadier-Division Nordland* had decorated their provisionary underground bunker lodging as well as possible. "There was a Christmas tree, fresh spruce-twigs, tinsel and small items we had received in the recent field post parcels," according to the SS soldier. The *Waffen-SS* division consisted of foreign volunteers including Swedes, Danes, Norwegians, Finns and Dutchmen fighting the Bolshevist enemy at the Eastern front. Since the autumn, the division and the remnants of *Heeresgruppe Nord* had been surrounded in Kurland and cut off from the German front. The Germans and their allies put up a fierce defense and managed to repulse the Red Army time and again. On New Year's Eve the men had a temporary respite after heavy fighting. They played cards at a table and listened to the new year's messages on the radio by the commanders of the various units. Christmas music was played as well.

Soldiers of the Volkssturm celebrate Christmas 1944 in a bunker in Eastern Prussia. On the table mail from the home front.
(Bundesarchiv, Bild 183-J28377 / CC-BY-SA 3.0)

In their primitive lodging, candlelight made shadows of the men on the damp walls. "By New Year's Eve," Wallin wrote after the war, "it was still looking as homely as it could be in a temporary underground bunker. Soldiers' rough, chapped and frozen hands had tenderly and carefully conjured up this Christmas treasure for all to share. We still cared for such [things] in the days between Christmas and New Year." Every now and then, one of the men took a swig from one of the canteens on the stove containing steaming glogg, the "Nordic version of English mulled and spiced wine." The sound of the radio was intermittently interrupted by some lively comments on the card game, or by a violent snore from one of the comrades.

That night, Wallin had to leave the relatively comfortable bunker for a reconnaissance patrol along front positions of the Red Army. The landscape, illuminated by a clear moon, had been transformed into a winter wonderland. "In the reflected whiteness of the cold sparkling snow, all outlines appeared razor sharp," the Swede recalled. "A group of trees, riddled by bullets and shells, with their splintered trunks and twisted network of branches, reminded me of grotesque figures in a fairy-tale about brownies and hobgoblins." When he arrived at a machine gun post manned by two men, he heard wild shooting over on the Soviet side. Drunken Red Army soldiers heralded the New Year in this way. A mere 50 metres from Wallin and the two other soldiers, on the far side of a railway embankment, there was a forward post of the Red Army. Conversations in Russian and the sound of a mouth organ were clearly audible.

"Comrade, why are you so melancholy?" suddenly sounded from the other side in broken German. "Did you get cabbage soup for dinner today, again?" It was the first time that the three men heard a Red Army soldier talk to them from across no man's land. They laughed about it and answered the question by firing their machine gun, followed by other automatic weapons in the vicinity. "Why do you shoot, comrade?" the same voice asked from the other side. The SS-soldier with the machine gun replied, "If you come over here and play the mouth organ for us, I will not shoot any more." In the bright moonlight Wallin and his comrades next saw a head emerge, clearly outlined against the gleaming white background in the wide open doors of a derailed freight car that had fallen over. "Then, a pair of shoulders appeared and indeed, there came a Red Army soldier in full view, struggling towards the railway embankment. Another two followed."

Soviet Christmas card from 1944, the text reads:
Granddaddy Frost makes his frightful round with Old and New so all that
Fascist scum shall disappear forever.

The Soviet soldiers attempted to climb onto the truck but they probably had had a little too much vodka under their belts to make it. The *Waffen-SS* soldiers had drunk alcohol as well, including wine from their Christmas parcels which added to the friendly atmosphere. On their side of the truck, one of the Ivans played his mouth organ while on the other side a soldier did a little dance which he could not keep up for long because of the rhythm of the melody, although it did help against the cold. After a Soviet soldier had cracked a dirty joke, answered by laughs from both sides, the Red Army soldiers disappeared from view.

Wallin's superior had learned about the incident and could laugh about it, but he forbade any more fraternization. The reputation of the *Waffen-SS* as fanatic anti-Bolshevists was at stake. When their superior had gone, the men on both fronts made contact again. They tried to outdo each other with the presents they had received for Christmas. Despite Christmas having been "abolished" by their regime, the Soviet soldiers also had received something extra from their home front, but they could not beat the present received by one of Wallin's mates. The man had been sent a pair of slippers by an old lady. "*Tufli, tufli,*" the Red Army soldiers yelled who, according to Wallin, had never heard of slippers "in the Soviet 'paradise' of workers and farmers," until it was explained to them by one of Wallin's mates who spoke a little Russian.

When they had lost the competition for who had received the finest Christmas present, the Soviet soldiers became "rude and insulting," according to the Swede. "They asked for the addresses of girls in Berlin they would soon be paying a visit." After further insults about Hitler and Stalin had been exchanged, a Soviet soldier tried to trade a pack of German tobacco for four packs of Russian tobacco. "They both climbed out of their trenches and approached each other. ... Just as they were within reach of each other, a bullet whistled past from a guard further away, who did not know of the situation, and had seen the two figures. They ran away from each other with giant leaps and disappeared under cover, as flashes came from different directions." After this, the rest of the night remained calm.

The next morning, mortars of Wallin's unit would bombard the Soviet lines.[26] On January 25, 1945, *Heeresgruppe Nord* was renamed *Heeresgruppe Kurland* and would hold out until the German capitulation on May 8, 1945. The Germans, however, paid a high price of at least 150,000 dead and wounded during the defense of this isolated front.[27] It was a clear example of the senseless self-destruction resulting from Hitler's refusal to accept the fact that the downfall of his Thousand Year Reich was imminent.

Notes chapter IV:

[1] Liese, H. (ed.), *Deutsche Kriegsweihnacht*, pp. 106-108.
[2] Liese, H. (ed.), *Deutsche Kriegsweihnacht*, pp. 8-10.
[3] Liese, H. (ed.), *Deutsche Kriegsweihnacht*, pp. 125-127.
[4] Bytwerk, R., 'Much Grain Grows during Winter's Night...', German Propaganda Archive Calvin College.
[5] Liese, H. (ed.), *Deutsche Kriegsweihnacht*, p. 190.
[6] Perry, J., 'Nazifying Christmas: Political Culture and Popular Celebration in the Third Reich', *Central European History*, Dec. 2005.
[7] Gajek, E., 'Christmas under the Third Reich', *Anthropology today*, nr. 6, 1990.
[8] Perry, J., *Christmas in Germany*, pp. 235-237; Gajek, E., 'Christmas under the Third Reich', *Anthropology today*, nr. 6, 1990.
[9] Rue, L., 'Potatoes Main Food in Seized German Towns', *Chicago Tribune*, 24 Dec. 1944.
[10] Engelke, J., 'Wie die Berliner in den dunkelsten Stunden feierten, Kriegsweihnacht 1944', *B.Z. Berlin*, 19 Dec. 2004.
[11] Vogt, H.R., *My Memories of Berlin: A Young Boy's Amazing Survival Story*, p. 218.
[12] Vogt, H.R., *My Memories of Berlin: A Young Boy's Amazing Survival Story*, pp. 241-242.
[13] Winterberg, S. & Winterberg, Y., *Kriegskinder: Erinnerungen einer Generation*, p. 150.
[14] Engelke, J., 'Wie die Berliner in den dunkelsten Stunden feierten, Kriegsweihnacht 1944', *B.Z. Berlin*, 19 Dec. 2004.
[15] Ballhausen, H., *Chronik des Zweiten Weltkriegs*, p. 448.
[16] König, W. von, *Wolfhilde's Hitler Youth Diary 1939-1946*.
[17] Ast, W.F., 'Seeing the war through the eyes of a Hitler Youth', *The Herald Palladium*, 28 Feb. 2013; König, W. von, *Wolfhilde's Hitler Youth Diary 1939-1946*.
[18] Ring, J., *Storming the Eagle's Nest: Hitler's War in the Alps*, p. 142.
[19] Hunt, I.A., *Op schoot bij Hitler*, pp. 190-195.
[20] Longerich, P., *Heinrich Himmler*, pp. 715, 718-719.
[21] Himmler, K. & Wildt, M., *Heinrich Himmler privé*, p. 284.
[22] Lippmann, I., 'Unsere letzte Weihnacht in Königsberg 1944', Lebendiges Museum Online, Apr. 2001.
[23] Fuhr, E., 'Wie Hitler sein letztes Weihnachtsfest verbrachte', *Welt*, 16 Dec. 2014.
[24] Fricke, B., '1944: Stille Nacht, unheilige Nacht, Weihnachten auf der Flucht', *Berliner Morgenpost*, 24 Dec. 2010.
[25] Bornemann, J. & Breunig, A. & Wirths, G., *Zwischen Franken und der Front*, pp. 77-78.

[26] Rogers, D. & Williams, S.R., *On the Bloody Road to Berlin: Frontline Accounts from North-West Europe and the Eastern Front, 1944-1945*, pp. 119-126.

[27] Grier, D., *Hitler, Donitz, and the Baltic Sea: The Third Reich's Last Hope, 1944-1945*, p. 74.

- V -
The Pearl of the Danube

Shortly before Christmas, Edó, a resident of Budapest, came home with "a splendid Christmas tree" that he had bought at a price far lower than in peace time. "Just take it," the woman had told him, "it does not matter anymore, the Russians are already in Budakeszi." The fact that the Red Army had actually reached the city west of the Hungarian capital was not taken seriously by Edó and his family. They thought the woman was exaggerating because Radio Budapest was still broadcasting Christmas carols played on an organ.

Elsewhere in town, nobody took an imminent Soviet siege into consideration. On December 23, in the municipal opera house, *Aida* was performed in a half-filled auditorium. Prior to the second act, an actor dressed as a soldier had come on stage to put the audience at ease: Budapest – the "Pearl of the Danube" – would remain Hungarian and the city had nothing to fear. In other theaters and cinemas, pre-Christmas shows continued as usual.[1]

The majority of the population of 1 million had remained in the city. The defense consisted of a garrison army of some 70,000 German and Hungarian soldiers, most of whom were billeted in Pest, the part of the city on the east bank of the Danube. In addition, there were paramilitary groups of the fascist Hungarian Arrow Cross Party. The quality of all units varied, and the numbers were not large enough to defend the Pearl of the Danube for any length of time.[2]

In December 1944, Budapest was not untouched by war. After the Hungarian head of state, Miklós Horthy, had made attempts to sign a separate peace with the Allies, Hitler had occupied his own ally's country on March 19, 1944, and on July 2 the capital was bombed by the Americans. Initially, Admiral Horthy had been allowed to remain in office, but when he made peace behind Hitler's back with the Soviet Union on October 11th, he was ousted and replaced by Ferenc Szálasi, chairman of the Arrow Cross Party. Szálasi introduced a reign of terror against the Jews who had stayed behind in the city after Horthy, under Allied pressure, on July 9 had stopped the deportations, which had started soon after the beginning of the German occupation in March.[3]

Non-Jewish opponents of Fascism had much to fear as well in the Hungary of Szálasi. One such person was the father of Magda Németh. She was 13 years old in 1944 and the eldest of four sisters. He was a writer, he taught biology, and just like many other Hungarian intellectuals he was critical of both Fascism and Communism. Due to his criticisms he spent a large part of 1944 in hiding. The family lived in a suburb of Buda – the part of the city on the west bank of the Danube – and lived in the countryside during the summer. In September, the family returned to the city. According to Magda, the atmosphere there had changed since March, with "German soldiers everywhere, destroyed buildings and rubble all over the city, alarmed people on the streets." The Soviet air force carried out air raids, and from the beginning of November on, the sound of heavy guns from the east came closer and closer.[4]

Since the summer, the Red Army had advanced relentlessly through Romania, Transylvania and eastern Hungary but was slowed down in October. Soviet leader Stalin wanted to capture the strategic city on both banks of the Danube as soon as possible in order to have a trump card in the negotiations with the Allies on the post-war spheres of influence. As early as November, the first T-34 tanks arrived in the eastern outskirts, but they were stopped short of the gates of Budapest by Hungarian defense, strongly supported by Germany. Reinforcements were rushed in from the city by tram. While these tactics prevented Budapest from being overrun in the east, Soviet troops advanced from both north and south on the city, and as a result, the city was completely surrounded. German and Hungarian troops were trapped and bombarded from all sides by 10,000 heavy artillery weapons. Hitler had ordered that the city be defended to the last stone but failed to send in reinforcements in time.[5] Contrary to all expectations, the city was invaded from the west as the Red Army reached the densely forested mountainous area on the outskirts of Buda on December 24. The area was defended by soldiers from a few trenches and bunkers, but they were unable to repel the attacks.[6]

One of the first signs of Stalin's army rapid approach to the center of the city was that tram service was suspended in the afternoon of December 24, when the Red Army captured a depot in Buda. A group of police officers and soldiers who went to see what was happening was subjected to enemy fire near Szent János Hospital. The Soviets had penetrated up to 2 miles from the majestic royal palace on the hill in Buda. Some Arrow Cross Party members and German citizens attempted to flee the city in panic, but the rest of the population could hardly be bothered by stories about the Soviet invasion. The public, by impassively doing their Christmas shopping, delayed the movement of German-Hungarian reinforcements to the west of the city.

One of the units which was ordered to take up positions in Buda was the *8. SS-Kavalerie-Division Florian Geyer,* which had had to abort its Christmas celebration in Pest.[7] The medical battalion of the unit had set up its major aid station in the wine cellar of the elegant Britannia Hotel. Apparently, the Hungarian elite remained unperturbed as mud-covered and bleeding soldiers were being carried past them through the dining hall.[8]

On December 24, 12 people had assembled in Magda Németh's house in Buda to celebrate Christmas. Magda's father had temporarily left his hiding place to be with them. Her mother had managed to obtain a Christmas tree and, with the ingredients she had saved, she made "a lovely dinner" for all of her guests. One of those present was a Hungarian captain who apparently had not understood the full scope of the military situation. While everyone sat at table waiting for the meal, the captain's adjutant ran in with the message that "there were Russian troops close by on the hill side." Dinner was cut short. "My mother put wine glasses and some pastries on a tray. If soldiers happened to knock at our door on Christmas Eve, she wanted to have something ready to offer to them," reported Magda, adding, "She still had an optimistic view of what we could expect."

Later that night they received confirmation from friends that the Red Army had arrived: "We tried to make a phone call to some friends down the hill. Surprisingly the phone worked and we were told that there were Russian troops everywhere, while tanks were rolling towards the city centre." The family decided that along with the other young women at the dinner, Magda and two of her sisters should go to the house of a friend of the family to be farther from the front and in a place where they would be safer from the Soviet soldiers. According to Magda, "The reputation of the invading troops had preceded them and made everyone fearful of the threat of rape." With a few Christmas presents and some things for the night, they set off in the darkness. Although they heard rifle fire from close by, they arrived at their destination unharmed.[9]

While some residents of Budapest feared the arrival of the Soviet soldiers, just as Magda did, and even stashed away their Christmas trees because they were afraid the atheist enemy would take offense, others were elated. From his apartment in the castle district of Buda, liberal politician Imre Csécsy compared the stuttering of machine guns to "the most beautiful Christmas music." For some Jews in hiding in the town, the arrival of the Red Army meant their survival. For example, Arrow Cross Party thugs were ready to murder the children hiding in a Jewish children's home on Budakeszi Road, but when the thundering Soviet guns approached, the thugs left without harming the children.[10]

The Örangyalház convent – Home of the Guardian Angel – was on the hill of the Buda citadel. There Swedish diplomat Raoul Wallenberg had sheltered about 100 Jewish women and children. They were entrusted to the care of the nuns under the direction of Mother Superior Klára Ráth. A priest declared about her: "She had a strong personality and could not be shaken…. she saved people through the front door and when that was impossible she brought them in through the window." On Christmas 1944 all the children slept in the cellar for their own safety. On Christmas Day they did not have to go to school and spent their time playing and reading. One of the girls, Zsuzsa Spiegel Layton, missed her mother very much, but according to her "the nuns were fantastic, very warm hearted." She remembered Christmas as "very beautiful, with the smell of pines … an enchanted atmosphere." Despite several raids on the convent during the occupation, Mother Klára managed to thwart all attempts by the Arrow Cross members to track down the children in the convent. She served alcohol to the men so they would forget their orders. Some ten years after her death, the mother superior was honored in 2010 with the title Righteous among the Nations by Yad Vashem, the World Holocaust Remembrance Center.[11]

In the spring of 1944 when Judit Grünfeld was seven, her father organized forged, non-Jewish identity papers for her. With the help of their good, loyal, Catholic friend, Mária Babar, Judit was sheltered in a convent. At some point her parents were deported to Bergen-Belsen. Arrow Cross harassment of Jews and the institutions sheltering them increased. Worried, Mária Babar took Judit away from the convent and home to her apartment in the Budapest suburb of Naphegy on the Castle Hill, together with her grandmother and an aunt who also had false identities. There, Judit celebrated a Christian

Christmas. In the "cramped, single room," where the three of them lived, Mária had put up "a real Christmas tree" which filled a large part of the room. The tree had been decorated with angels' hair and other glistening trinkets, but it was "the foil-wrapped traditional Hungarian Christmas candies hanging on its branches," that especially attracted the young girl's attention. She looked forward to tasting them and lighting the candles in the tree. Presents she had made herself for her family and friends were under the tree. "It was going to be better than a birthday party," Judit predicted. Although the food supply in the city was dwindling and meat and sugar were strictly rationed, the hostess did succeed in preparing a fine Christmas dinner. Judit did not know where her guardian got the food from or if she had dared to apply for ration cards for her guests in hiding. In any case she later thought that there were "some horseshoe-shaped poppy seed and sweet ground walnut-filled cakes that Jews called *beigli* and gentiles *patkó*."

On Christmas Eve, the women and their guests sang traditional Christmas carols, which were suddenly interrupted by the sound of explosions and the shrieking of air raid sirens throughout the city. From a window in Mária's apartment they saw the bridges on the Danube explode like fireworks. "From the Castle Hill, where the royal palace looked out over the destruction, guns were roaring," Judit continued her report about that evening. "Machine guns stuttered. Hand grenades exploded. Windows shattered. Air planes buzzed above us in clusters." The women and Judit fled to the provisional bomb shelter they had prepared in case of emergency. They had put mattresses on old iron bedsteads. Jars of preserved food were on shelves against the wall, "including duck, fried and packed in jars filled with duck fat – and tall brown jute sacks of flour, onions and potatoes." The Christmas presents remained upstairs however and were buried beneath the debris of the house which was turned into rubble by the violence of war. "The siege of Budapest had begun on my first and only Christmas," Judit said.[12]

The siege of the Hungarian capital would gain nowhere near the same reputation as, for instance, the siege of Leningrad or the entrapment of the German 6. *Armee* in Stalingrad, but in all its ferocity, it was a catastrophic battle as well, claiming tens of thousands of victims on both sides. What started on December 24 as local skirmishes on the outskirts of Buda, soon turned into a city-wide bloody battle which raged on even in the sewers. That day, Hitler would finally send reinforcements to Hungary, while in the streets of Budapest, barricades were erected.[13] Hungarian students and pupils reported as volunteers or were forcefully drafted into the army to help defend their city. The cooperation between German and Hungarian commanders left much to be desired, due to mutual distrust. Many Hungarians who would have nothing to do with the fascist Arrow Cross Party or the German occupier deserted to the Red Army, where an entire battalion could be made up with defectors. An appeal by the Soviet commander, Marshall Rodion Malinovsky, to surrender was rejected though.

While the city was subjected to artillery fire from all sides and Soviet bombers inflicted massive damage, many citizens hid in cellars and tunnels or in the system of limestone passageways beneath the Castle Hill. Without water, gas, electricity and sufficient food, their city turned into hell. Many citizens lost their lives while going to get water or standing in line at the soup kitchens.[14]

A few days after December 24, the home of the Németh family was requisitioned by the Germans to be used as an observation post. On December 28, the family took up residence in a students' home in the southern part of Buda where they were able to hide in the cellar during bombardments. That day, Magda's mother, on her way to the baker's shop, sustained a severe leg injury from shell fragments. She was taken to a hospital where there was a shortage of medicines. Towards year's end she lost consciousness. Her life was saved by a medic from the German division that was housed in the same building as her family. He extracted the fragments from her wounds, disinfected them and returned a few times to treat her injuries.

Meanwhile, Magda and the others went hungry. They often had soup from the field kitchen nearby. She had to get water from a pump on a square which was frequently under fire. With 400 people in the cellar and so many soldiers in the building above, the hygienic situation was deplorable. In January, members of the Arrow Cross also took up residence here. Men over 18 were forced to take up arms, but Mr. Németh and the other men in the group managed to flee to a partially demolished house belonging to a friend of the family. There they went into hiding. The women and children remained behind in the building which eventually was on the front line and had to endure strikes by bombs and shells.[15]

Like Stalingrad, the surrounded Budapest could be supplied only by air and by boat from across the Danube, although the latter was no longer possible after the end of January when the Danube froze over completely and was defended by the Soviets.[16] As the major airports had been occupied since December, emergency air strips were pressed into service, for instance, on a race track and on a training ground to accommodate the German Ju 52 transport aircraft.[17] Some of the supplies were dropped over the city by parachute. Despite all this, from January on, decreasing amounts of food were available for the military and civilians alike. Rations usually consisted of meat from slaughtered army horses and watery soup. Melted snow was used for drinking water. As a result of the poor living conditions, the defenders of the city were plagued by lice and diarrhea. In addition, they had to be constantly on guard against snipers and small infiltration units, out to make unwary soldiers prisoners of war or to kill them.

An attempt to break out – although forbidden by Hitler – by Hungarian and German soldiers on February 11 failed. On February 13, the defenders of the city finally surrendered to the Red Army. This did not immediately end the suffering of the civilian population as gangs of plundering, raping and murdering Soviet soldiers caused much distress.[18]

The building where Magda Németh and her mother and sisters had moved after Christmas was captured by Soviet soldiers on February 2. They fled to the cellar beneath the house of the friend where her father had found shelter before. It was cold, and, for lack of better food, they ate the meat of a horse that a Soviet soldier had killed because it was injured. Their own house was destroyed, and the neighborhood was terrorized by gangs of plundering and raping Soviet military men.

When the battle was finally over, the family moved in March to a village in the countryside in eastern Hungary where there was still sufficient food. It was an exhausting journey. They crossed the Danube, full of ice floes, in a small and heavily laden boat. They were in constant fear of being arrested and deported by the Soviets. When they finally arrived at the family which received them, they were overjoyed. They were given a large room, "clean clothes and a hot bath. ... When we were cleaned up, a magnificent dinner lasting hours was waiting for us," Magda clearly remembered dozens of years later. "This was in the middle of March, and we had not seen proper food since Christmas Eve."[19]

Between Christmas and February, Judit, the young girl in hiding, hardly ever emerged above ground. Only much later did she learn that her shelter had been located in the suburb where the Germans held out the longest. During the heavy fighting, the building above collapsed and electricity was cut, so they had to light the cellar with candles and kerosene lamps. Judit, Mária and her aunt dared to venture outside only when the battle was over and the city officially liberated by the Soviets. "It was February 1945 and all that was left of the apartment we had abandoned on Christmas Eve was a pile of rubble," Judit said years later. "There was no time to regret lost things. We were alive."

During a walk with Mária, she saw how the once romantic old city had been transformed into a massive scene of destruction. The women had to cross the Danube on an emergency bridge as "the once-graceful arches spanning the river were tangles of twisted metal on broken stone pillars." On the way, they saw "houses razed to the ground or cut in half, grotesque cross-sections with pieces of furniture and wall paintings that appeared to hang in mid-air." Notably, the apartment of her mother's family in a fashionable suburb of Pest was undamaged other than a few bullet holes in the exterior wall. Judit took up residence here with her aunt and grandmother, and "life began to assume some normalcy."[20]

Notes chapter V

[1] Ungváry, K., *Battle for Budapest: 100 Days in World War II*, pp. 40, 51.

[2] Groot, B. de, 'World War II: Siege of Budapest', Historynet.com, 06 Dec. 2006.

[3] Beevor, A., *De Tweede Wereldoorlog*, pp. 712-713.

[4] Németh, M., 'During and after the Siege of Budapest (1944-1945), *Hungarian Review*, 14 Jan. 2015.

[5] Beevor, A., *De Tweede Wereldoorlog*, p. 742-1743; Mitcham, S.W. jr., *The German Defeat in the East, 1944-45*, pp. 231,235.

[6] Ungváry, K., *Battle for Budapest: 100 Days in World War II*, p. 40.

[7] Groot, B. de, 'World War II: Siege of Budapest', Historynet.com, 06 Dec. 2006.

[8] Mitcham, S.W. jr., *The German Defeat in the East, 1944-45*, p. 237.

[9] Németh, M., 'During and after the Siege of Budapest (1944-1945), *Hungarian Review*, 14 Jan. 2015.

[10] Ungváry, K., *Battle for Budapest: 100 Days in World War II*, pp. 49, 52.

[11] 'Rescue Story Ráth, Klára', Database of Righteous Among The Nations.

[12] 'Judy Abrams: Tenuous Threads', The Azrieli Series Short Films.

[13] Groot, B. de, 'World War II: Siege of Budapest', Historynet.com, 06 Dec. 2006.

[14] Beevor, A., *De Tweede Wereldoorlog*, p. 744; Groot, B. de, 'World War II: Siege of Budapest', Historynet.com, 06 Dec. 2006.

[15] Németh, M., 'During and after the Siege of Budapest (1944-1945), *Hungarian Review*, 14 Jan. 2015.

[16] Groot, B. de, 'World War II: Siege of Budapest', Historynet.com, 06 Dec. 2006.

[17] Ungváry, K., *Battle for Budapest: 100 Days in World War II*, p. 62.

[18] Beevor, A., *De Tweede Wereldoorlog*, p. 749; Groot, B. de, 'World War II: Siege of Budapest', Historynet.com, 06 Dec. 2006.

[19] Németh, M., 'During and after the Siege of Budapest (1944-1945), *Hungarian Review*, 14 Jan. 2015.

[20] 'Judy Abrams: Tenuous Threads', The Azrieli Series Short Films; Abrams, J. & Felsenburg Marx, E., *Tenuous Threads / One of the Lucky Ones*.

- VI -
Light in the Darkness

It was cold in the military vehicles that were driving towards the Mount Saint Peter near Maastricht in the evening of December 24, 1944. The American soldiers inside felt the biting cold on their hands and feet. On the way to their final destination, they got lost on the dark roads which made them afraid of being too late. They arrived ahead of time, however, and they would never forget the experience of that night. "We never had such a lovely Mass in a most appropriate place for a Christmas Mass," one of them stated.[1]

Maastricht had been liberated by American troops on September 14, 1944. The Dutch city in Limburg Province was spared a battle as most Germans had already disappeared. Some 800 Americans were tasked with maintaining public order and security. Catholic chaplain Dobrzynski saw to the spiritual wellbeing of the troops. With Christmas on the horizon, he came up with the idea to celebrate the Holy Mass in a special place. He had selected a marl cave under the Sint Pietersberg as its location. It was owned by the Friars of Maria Immaculate Conception, a monastic order founded in 1840 which is better known in Maastricht as the Brothers of the Beyart.

The marl cave was named De Schark after the country estate to which it belonged. Following the liberation of Maastricht, soldiers were billeted in the country house of the monks. A large hall was in use as a mess. Two soldiers slept in a tent outside in the bitter cold to guard the ammunition. Other Americans were billeted in a school where monks were also housed in the cellar because a wing of the monastery had been destroyed by bombs on September 17, 1944. Consequently, the Americans and the monks were no strangers to each other, and it probably took the American priest only a little persuasion to get the monastic order to support his idea. Magister Lidwino de Koning, the superior, gave his permission. The responsible American general also approved, although the Mass nearly had been cancelled, because of the Ardennes offensive that had erupted on December 16th. During the service, two soldiers would stand guard for security reasons.[2]

One corridor in the cave had been prepared by the monks for the gathering. An altar had been constructed from marlstone with a mural behind it depicting shepherds receiving the message of the birth of Jesus from the angels. An American soldier drew a picture of the liberation of Europe on another wall. A third wall was reserved for the Americans to write their signatures at the end of the mass. To complete the interior of the temporary chapel, an organ was moved from the monastery to the cave. During the celebration, the instrument would be played by monks as well as by an American soldier. Towards 23:00 hours, the monks were collected by two army trucks, escorted by MPs on motorcycles, two up front and two in the rear. It was pitch dark and desolate in the city. While on the road, the air raid siren sounded. The convoy was stopped twice by military for inspection.

Corporal Allan J. English of the 127 AA Battalion, an anti-aircraft unit, and his mates were also on their way to the cave on this cold and dark night. Despite his fears of being late, he arrived fifty minutes ahead of time for the service. In a letter to his mother, written a day later, he described how he entered the cave and reached the subterranean chapel, illuminated with small bulbs, through long corridors. He was impressed by "the beautiful charcoal murals on the walls and the sculptured pillars, corridors, rooms, and the whole place seemed like a piece of art. ... It was a place not to be found anywhere else in the world."[3]

English was one of about 260, mostly young, Americans who met in the cave. Some soldiers had been transferred from the front to recuperate for a while. "They were all armed, their guns at the ready," Friar Lucianus, one of the almost thirty monks present, declared in the *Limburgs Dagblad* in 2012. "It might just happen they had to scramble. We were also told beforehand that the service might have to be aborted in the middle of the celebration. You did feel the pressure of war." As they entered, the choir of young monks sang the Christmas carol "Adeste Fideles," better known in English as "Oh Come All Ye Faithful." After opportunity had been given for confessions, the real celebration began. "It was a superb gathering," Friar Lucianus said. "A magnificent atmosphere. So quiet, so intense. It was so... so real. It is about the birth of Christ and then you find yourself in a cave! It was romantic but we also were well aware of the seriousness of the matter."[4]

At the conclusion of the religious service, an American played the American national anthem, followed by other songs which, according to one of the friars, had little to do with Christmas. Next, the Americans wrote their names or signatures with charcoal on the designated wall. At the end of the service, their general entered the cave and also signed his name on the wall. He was not a Catholic. That would also have applied to others of those present, yet they all enjoyed this special Christmas celebration which, according to one of the Americans, was reminiscent of the Christmas celebration at home. Apart from the soldiers, two boys from Maastricht had been present at the Mass although this was actually forbidden. According to one of the friars, at the end the participants were treated to "a mug of hot coffee and cream, a spoonful of powdered sugar and a large, nutritious doughnut." Some Americans had left immediately after Mass and so they missed out on these treats.[5]

American military write their names on the wall of the Schark Cave.
(U.S. Army via: www.shak1944.org)

When the service was over, the soldiers went back to their quarters, as did the monks, who went on to celebrate the Midnight Mass once more in their monastery. Some soldiers, who had come from the Ardennes in their trucks, were driven straight back to the front after Christmas Eve. Today, the chapel in the cave is an official American memorial site. Apart from the wall with names, there are some reliefs and a plaque in memory of the Second World War. Over the years since the war, various American veterans have returned to the cave to remember the Christmas celebration they looked back on with warm feelings.[6]

Outside of Maastricht, Christmas 1944 was celebrated in freedom in other locations in the Netherlands as well. In December 1944, the Allied front ran along the river Meuse for the most part with a salient in the direction of Arnhem as a result of Operation Market Garden. After fierce battles in the fall in the Scheldt estuary and on the island of Walcheren, the province of Zeeland was also liberated, except for Schouwen-Duiveland.[7]

Liberation, however, did not always mean the end of the violence of war, as fighting was still raging along the front line. Coba Jansen from Nijmegen was looking forward to celebrating Christmas with the Canadian liberators. Like many families in town she had invited a number of soldiers to join her for Christmas dinner. When, before Christmas, fierce fighting broke out on the front near Berg en Dal in Gelderland, she saw her chances dwindle. At seven o'clock on Christmas Eve, the doorbell rang. At the door were two Canadian soldiers whom she had befriended, together with their Irish friend. They entered with gleaming faces, in filthy battledress and heavily armed. As a Christmas present for the family, they had brought white bread, butter and other treats. The threesome had permission to leave the front in a jeep for a short while to tell her they were unable to make it on Christmas Day. Their Dutch friends immediately took out the Christmas cake and the presents for them. The men saved the parcels for the next day. After a cozy evening, the soldiers left at 23:30 hours. It was clear outside and there was a full moon. Only the bright exhaust flames of a V-1, clearly outlined against the starry sky, made it clear that there was still a war going on.[8]

For an unnamed, 18-year-old secretary from Eindhoven who worked for the British intelligence service, Christmas was "marvelous" and "unforgettable". She attended Holy Mass, which had been postponed from midnight until 05:30 hours because of the curfew. She was happy the church was no longer blacked out. After Mass, there was breakfast with old-fashioned sausage rolls (an old Brabant tradition), and she sang Christmas carols with her sisters. She went to bed at 10:00 and rose after lunch to go skating with her friend, a British captain she called "Carr", who came to fetch her in his jeep. "It was heaven, the first ice of the year," she wrote in Dutch in her diary. That night, her mother prepared "tinned chicken and a more than delicious hare" for their Christmas dinner. "No, I have never had such a delicious hare in my life."[9]

Christmas dinner was also better than ever for Annie van Stipthout, 12 years of age when her home town of Tilburg was liberated on October 27, 1944. Prior to Christmas, Annie and her sister had made Christmas cards and calendars for the Scottish soldiers billeted in her house. They bought picture postcards at V&D (a large department store) which they decorated with red, white and blue ribbons and orange strings. The gifts were eagerly accepted by the soldiers, who in return gave cigarettes, chocolate and soap. Some of the soldiers presented the girls with edible items like bread, corned beef and coffee creamer. They could be put to good use as their father suffered from double pneumonia which he had incurred while gathering food. It was expected he would die, but thanks to the additional food he was able to regain his strength and was cured. When Annie wished a Merry Christmas to the Scots, who woke up the neighborhood each day with their bagpipe music, they took her and two friends to their lodging for a surprise. In the dining room there was a table filled with all sorts of goodies, including roast turkey – a dish the young girl did not know at all. In addition there were roulades, Christmas stollen (a Dutch traditional sweet bread filled with raisins and almond paste), cakes and pudding. According to Annie, it was "just like being in heaven." She had never known such abundance during and probably even before the occupation.[10]

The Canadian tank commander Bob Elliott had been involved in the liberation with his 19th Field Regiment and was stationed in Alphen aan de Maas during Christmas 1944. He was shocked by the poverty, the anxiety and the suffering of the Dutch population. The young man from the small village of Olds in Alberta Province was only fifteen years old when he voluntarily signed up for the Canadian army because he did not want to lag behind his two elder brothers who already were in the army.[11] Actually, he was too young, "but when you looked strong and mature, they would look the other way," he stated later.[12] On D-Day, June 6, 1944 he went ashore in Normandy with his tank. When he had to stop on the beach because too many dead and wounded were lying in the way, his vehicle was hit by a German anti-tank shell. Two of his crew members were killed and the tank burned out completely. Only later that night did he notice that he had lost the tip of a finger when the shell struck.[13] With a new tank, he participated in the advance through France and Belgium and the liberation of Zeeland. In November 1944 he ended up in Alphen aan de Maas where he was deployed in the so-called winter line where the Allies were taking up positions to continue the advance after the winter and to prevent the Germans from crossing the River Maas (Meuse).

The soldiers, who were deployed in the flood plains near Alphen, attracted the attention of ten-year old Sussie Cretier who lived in an old farm nearby with her parents and two brothers. The family came from Rossum originally but were forced to flee after the Germans had found out that Sussie's father, Willem Cretier, was active in the resistance, passing on information to the Allies. Despite having the Germans close on their heels and having been under their fire during their escape, all family members managed to reach Alphen un-harmed. Her father was a mechanic and he liked to tinker with the tanks of the Canadians.[14]

Sussie could also often be found among the soldiers and did not escape the attention of Bob Elliott. After the war he remembered clearly how the little girl was eager to see the inside of a tank. She was put on top of a tank and did not let herself be deterred – with her fingers in her ears – when the Canadians fired the gun. According to the Canadian veteran, she, wide-eyed, asked him and the other soldiers for chocolate and chewing gum for herself and cigarettes for her father – all of which the Canadians were only too glad to give her.[15] A special friendship developed between the girl and the sol-diers. For them, her laughing, singing and her presence meant a cheerful distraction from the war. Their gifts were big treats to the family who lived in poor conditions and suffered from hunger and cold.[16]

When they escaped from Rossum, the Cretiers had only been able to take a minimum of luggage with them. The clothes Sussie had were worn-out and badly needed replacement. Therefore Elliot and his   mates decided to surprise the girl on Christmas with new cloth-ing. The men found an old woman who tailored a coat out of a grey army blanket with a double row of golden buttons they had taken from their own uniforms.[17] Everyone chipped in some money so that two Canadians could buy leather shoes, a sweater and a scarf for their young "mascot" when they were on leave in Paris. When she had been sent to get milk on Christmas morning, the Canadians called her in.[18] According to Elliot, Sussie was overjoyed, and her mother got tears in her eyes on seeing her little daughter in her new clothing.[19]

After that, every Tuesday, when the soldiers were cleaning their weapons and polishing their buttons and shoes, Sussie polished hers, until the Canadians left in the direction of Germany in February 1945. After the war, Bob kept in touch with the Cretier family, and in 1981 he paid them a short visit. Sussie met the Canadian at Schiphol Airport. They immediately recognized each other and sparks flew. They had both been divorced, and they married each other soon after the reunion.[20] Today, the small coat, a token of the friendship and lasting bond between the Netherlands and Canada, is on public display in the Canadian War Museum in Ottawa.[21]

The Christmas period did not proceed undisturbed for Toke Dankers-van Beek. The diary writer, born April 24, 1918, lived in 1944 on Morgenrust Farm in Dongen in Noord-Brabant. Dongen might well have been liberated in October, but the war remained a daily reality. The place lay exactly below the flight path of V-1 bombs that were fired from the occupied Netherlands against Antwerp. On December 20, the woman wrote in her diary that on that day two people had been killed when a V-1 crashed into a house in nearby Kaatsheuvel. "All day long, those things fly past," she wrote "and we are very much afraid in case their motor stops and they can come down at any moment."

On December 23, Toke's fear became reality: the motor of a V-1 fell off above their house. "What distress," she wrote. "In no time we were on our knees in the water as we were mopping the kitchen floor at the back and expected the bomb to hit our house at any moment. But after a few anxious minutes we dared go out and look where it was, and fortunately it flew on. That was quite a relief, but the broom still shook in my hands as it moved over the tiles. The next day, the bombs flew past more than ever." On Christmas Eve there were, she wrote, "surely three every ten minutes" and a few came down in the area. Moreover, on the distant front, there was more shooting than ever. "The guns roared continuously at fifteen-minute intervals, making so much noise nobody could have slept a wink. What a difference from other Christmas Eves that are usually so intensely quiet and radiating peace."

At 06:00 in the morning, she attended Holy Mass, where prayers for peace were said. Through the freezing cold she returned home, where a Christmas stable, a decorated Christmas table and burning candles created a real Christmas-like atmosphere. Toke however felt the utmost joy because of the real coffee that had not been in her home for four years, but now, thanks to a distribution of coffee ration cards, it could be brewed again. "It was a very good cup, mind you," she told her diary. During the day, more than a dozen people skated on the pond behind the house. The fun was over when around 16:00 shooting was heard and aircraft were buzzing in the sky above. Toke and the other skaters dived onto the ice, "flat on our stomachs as bullets struck less than 30 feet away from us. What a shock that was. A German bomber had taken the liberty to snoop around over the airfield (probably Gilze-Rijen) and was being pursued for a while by three fighters."

During the rest of the year, it still did not remain quiet in Dongen. The Allies deployed heavy guns in the area, and the roaring of cannons resulted in windows "being blown out with frames and all." On December 29, a V-1 crashed in a field one kilometer from the Van Beek farm, making the house shake, and blowing out four window panes. "Almost all houses on the Vaart [Road] here are damaged, even in Dongen," she wrote. "The roofing tiles on the new barn were all scattered everywhere, as if a hurricane had passed." On New Year's Eve, Allied fighters flew past continuously, and the next night guns were roaring. There was fighting going on near Capelle where the Germans defended their bridgehead across the Bergsche Maas canal until January 31, 1945.[22]

A little further on, in the hamlet of Oosteind between Dongen and Oosterhout, seven-year old Ad Jansen wandered curiously among the 2,000 Canadians who had been billeted here. The soldiers had filled the main road in the village with artillery pieces targeting the front near the Bergsche Maas. Along with other children, the boy was allowed to help the Canadians prepare their Christmas celebration. The children gathered Christmas branches in the forest for decorating a barn. A Christmas tree completed it. On Christmas Eve, Ad and his brother and sister were put in their box-bed early as they had to get up at 03:30 the next morning to be on time for Holy Mass in the church. He had only slept a short while when all hell broke loose as the hundreds of guns started firing at the German line. The children became very, very afraid. Their parents had got out of their own box-bed, and Ad thought they were praying near the stove, "as they too were frightened to death." They feared the Germans would return.

"It was such a nightmare," he declared in an interview after the war, "in particular those bangs of the guns ... were so ear-shattering that after a while you could not hear anything anymore, nothing more than just those bangs and then the whistling that followed.... You heard nothing else but those bangs. Then the reverberation of the house after such an explosion. The rattling of doors and of the planks that had been nailed over the window openings because all panes had already disappeared due to the shooting, due to the pressure waves."

When Ad and his family went to church early the next morning, the gunfire had only slightly abated. It was still dark, and each time a shell was fired, the whole street was lit up as if it were broad daylight. Overwhelmed by the noise, the family walked to the church. In Ad's words, "it was a walk of almost half an hour and I still remember we were walking like robots for you could not talk, of course, as there was nothing you could understand. You could only hold hands and support each other." When they entered the church and the mass started about fifteen minutes later, the shooting finally stopped. "And when ... the organ began to play; now that sounded like something heavenly to me, something from another world, something that did not belong in this world any more. It was so very beautiful, because all during the night you had heard nothing else but the heavy drumming and howling of the guns that you really thought that other sounds were not possible anymore. And when shortly after one of my cousins started singing 'Silent Night' it felt like a celebration."[23]

The major part of the Netherlands, however, still had to wait for liberation that Christmas. To the north of the great rivers, the German occupation was still a daily reality. Across the Bergsche Maas, in the Land of Heusden and Altena, the German forces were assembling prior to Christmas. According to 35-year-old school teacher Mrs. Verhorst, "a nervous, agitated atmosphere prevailed in the village of Almkerk." As more and more Germans moved in, quartermasters went from house to house to requisition sleeping space. According to the woman, "the Germans dragged along the most fantastic means of transport, including old prams," because "nothing much is left of a mechanized army."

In the house where the teacher rented a room, Germans were also billeted. In the small room of two NCOs, a "brand new map of France was pinned to the wall – the branch of a fir tree above it." The woman was afraid the troops that were assembling in the area were preparing to cross the Bergsche Maas and advance into France in support of the Ardennes offensive. "*Wir gehen wieder nach Breda, nach*

Frankreich!" (we're going back to Breda, to France), a sergeant yelled, confirming the woman's fears. But it would not come to that, and on Christmas the Germans were still in the village. Shortly before Christmas, there was much German activity in the streets, but this clearly had to do with celebrating the holiday. Mrs. Verhorst saw "trucks, field kitchens and other vehicles with hay and straw on which were geese they wanted to slaughter for their Christmas dinner." Soldiers also "carried meat and schnapps and all sorts of other things in order to throw that party."

The Germans who slept under the same roof as the teacher celebrated Christmas as well. On the evening of Boxing Day (December 26) and the following night, they made far too much noise. While the woman and the other residents of the house had sought shelter in the cellar (the front line was a mere 6 miles away), the Germans were throwing a party in their room, not only on the occasion of Christmas but also because of the birthday of one of them. They had hoarded enough schnapps, had invited their friends, and there also was at least one woman. The party started at 19:00 and after an hour, they were all roaring drunk, according to the teacher. In the cellar, they could hear the Germans sing and yell, interrupted by the hysterical laughing of a woman – "a *moffenhoer*" (a Dutch woman fraternizing with Germans). "And that lasted the whole night through," according to the teacher; "every now and then they attempted to sing a Christmas carol but they failed of course."

At 02:00 they heard banging on the outer door and a voice calling in German that the party should be over now. The guests left, and the others stumbled up the stairs to their sleeping quarters. The furious landlady immediately left the cellar to inspect the mess the Germans had made. She sternly watched one of the men, "his sleeves rolled up" mopping the corridor where it was a "terrible mess." The man "did not dare to say anything else.... As drunk as he was from the booze, he was just as sober from fear.... He cleaned things up as much as possible, disappeared into his room and we did not hear them anymore. The next day however, they avoided us a little because they felt a little uneasy about the noise they had made."[24]

To the west of the Land of Heusden and Altena and hemmed in by rivers lies the Biesbosch, a tidal area that connects to the North Sea by the Hollands Diep and the Haringvliet. Formally, the area lay in occupied territory, but it took the Germans much trouble and effort to secure the area which was filled with creeks, patches of reed, and willow forests. They hardly ever ventured into large parts of the marshy area, accessible only through narrow channels, because they feared geting lost or being ambushed by the resistance that was active here. Because the area was located between occupied and liberated territory, members of the resistance used it as an important crossing to transfer information, medicines, and Allied aircrews. The operators of these so-called line crossings knew the labyrinth inside out and maintained the crossings with canoes and row boats, with the villages of Werkendam and Sliedrecht as their launching points. One of those line-crossers was Cornelis Pieter van den Hoek from Werkendam. The leadership of their resistance group had selected him and his mate Arie van Driel to make a crossing on Christmas Eve carrying microfilms containing important information for the Allies. They did not exactly feel like it, as there were better – and warmer – ways to spend Christmas Eve, but duty called.

The men set off from Werkendam with Drimmelen as their final destination, a journey of some 2.5 to 3 hours they made in a *korjaal*, a type of canoe with an outboard motor. They had to row the whole way as the sound of the motor would surely betray them. They made the outbound journey at low tide and the journey home at high tide, which made rowing easier. On the way, they would have to be on their guard continuously as the Germans patrolled with *Schnellbooten* – fast boats – and had established machine gun nests on the banks. "When you came to a creek," Van Hoek explained, "there could be a boat full of Germans lying there. So you were under pressure for 2½ to 3 hours before you got to the far side. The only thing that might betray you were ducks in the reeds."

The two from Werkendam preferred to sail on dark and moonless nights, preferably in a bit of rough weather with a little rain if possible. Now such conditions were out of the question, but because of the activities and the Ardennes offensive it was rather quiet in the Biesbosch. During the journey, they could hear the roar of the Canadian guns on the far side of the river. "It was all crackling and howling, and, well, you did not really know what you heard. "While the resistance fighter thought "about the birth of Jesus," he wondered about the fact that there was no Christmas truce. The Canadian shelling of the Land of Heusden and Altena provided them with sufficient cover. That night, they had "a relatively quiet crossing," and later on both men returned safely.[25]

Some 12.5 miles to the west, three other men spent Christmas night in a bed of willows on Hoeksche Waard Island near Strijen. They had become stuck there while they were on their way to cross over to the Allied lines. One of them was the young resistance fighter Bernard 'Ben' Beukema who was on his way south to get blank ID cards that could be used to provide false identities for people in hiding. He also was in possession of military intelligence from Dordrecht that had to be delivered to the liberated territory. He had made two previous attempts to reach liberated Willemstad via the island of Tiengemeenten in the Haringvliet, but these had failed.

The third attempt was made on December 23, this time trying to cross the Hollands Diep near Strijen. Ben was not alone but with a group of about fourteen, including six guides, a number of Dutch resistance fighters, and an American and a Canadian pilot whose aircraft had crashed in enemy territory and who would rejoin their own people. All crossers assembled in the butcher shop in Strijen where they "wolfed down a delicious meal" and discussed their plans. They set off at 04:00 in weather that was actually unsuitable. A cold eastern wind had completely blown away the fog, and the polders and reeds were lit up by the moon which was sharply etched in the starry sky. Without darkness as a natural ally, the men had to be extremely cautious. In addition, more Germans than usual were patrolling the area. In fact, it was irresponsible to make the journey, but the men did not wish to delay any longer, and they were expected on the other side.

The first part of the route was covered on foot. They had to traverse a wide strip of land that had been flooded with water by the Germans between Strijen and Strijensas further to the south. They had to wade some 600 yards through the shallow water, step by step, making as little noise as possible. The icy water did not yet come to the top of their boots but their legs were getting very cold. After crossing this strip safely, the next obstacle was a swampy terrain next to a farm. Panic erupted here as their route was blocked by a German patrol. A loud *"Halt!"* sounded though the night. The men fled in all directions while the Germans opened fire on them. One of them was hit and died. Ben ran in the direction of the farm in order to hide there from the bullets that were whistling past him. On the run, he threw away everything he was carrying, including a bottle of milk and bread, unaware he would need them later on. He stumbled over a molehill and fell to the frozen ground, but he got up and immediately had to get down again as he was being shot at. Tracer bullets lit up the landscape. The young man, however, managed to find shelter in the undergrowth where he could catch his breath and make a plan. His situation seemed perilous: to return meant falling into the hands of the Germans, but continuing was senseless because he could not cross the Hollands Diep on his own.

When the shooting had diminished and the light of the tracer bullets had died down, Ben ran farther away from the Germans. After some 300 yards, he fell into a machine gun nest manned by a German soldier. The German might have been just as frightened as the Dutchman, who seemed to appear from nowhere. Ben soon managed to free himself from his perilous position and dived to the ground a few yards away from the position and opened fire on the German with his revolver. As the German ducked low, Ben ran to a bunch of reeds where he hoped to find cover. It was a mistake, however, as he landed in a mud puddle, risking sinking into the mud. As the mud sucked him down he grabbed at reed stems to pull himself up, losing one of his boots in the process. Trudging through the reeds, he was once again under fire. On his way he buried the military papers he was carrying in the marshy ground to prevent them from falling into German hands. Continuing, he reached some barren, swampy terrain where he saw someone standing. Cautiously, he moved up closer and saw it was not a German but one of the crossers, Bram de Jong, a resistance fighter from Rotterdam. In the reeds, someone else from their group was hiding as well – the guide Jurrie van der Linden. The three of them continued on their way.

Despite his role as a guide, Jurrie, like the others, failed to find the way through the wasteland where they found themselves. He decided they had to try to reach the small harbor of Strijensas. While shooting and calls of *"Halt!"* could still be heard in the distance, they reached a strip of reeds with the Hollands Diep behind it. At that moment, Ben was in a bad condition. His bare foot – his sock was still in the boot he lost – had been torn open by the sharp reed stems and it took him increasing effort to keep moving.

As day broke, the threesome hid in the dense reeds. They were close to their target, the Hollands Diep, and freedom winked, but they could not cross the river without a boat and without the cover of darkness. The first problem appeared to be resolved soon when Bram and Jurrie discovered a rowboat frozen among the reeds. They labored for hours to dig out the boat and drain the water out, but they could not move the heavy thing. In between efforts they shared some of the bread one of them was carrying and smoked a cigarette.

The attempts to get the boat out proved to be fruitless, and the three decided to move further into the willows and to try to return to the civilized world unseen. Ben had wrapped his scarf around his bare foot, which soon became frostbitten. Exhausted and thirsty, he trudged behind the other men. Time and again, they encountered open country full of German patrols. Dusk fell sooner than they had wished. Exhausted, they were left with no other option than to find a suitable bivouac and spend Christmas night in the willows.

A sheltered spot with some moss on the ground had to pass for their sleeping space. Ben and Jurrie crawled close to each other to share their body warmth while Bram went to sleep alone. They spent the freezing night with their hands beneath their clothing to protect them from frostbite. Their bodies stiffened and the next morning it took them a lot of effort to get out of their frozen positions. Even more exhausted than the day before, they set off again. They managed to cross a 30-foot wide creek on a raft made of a plank and willow branches. Jurrie, who could not swim, sat on the raft with the dry clothes of the other two men who pushed the raft forward by swimming. In the icy water, it felt like thousands of needles being stuck into their bodies. On the far bank, Ben and Bram dried themselves with their shirts and put their clothes back on. The cold water had been too much, though, for Bram. All color had drained from his face, saliva was dripping from his mouth, and he sank down on his knees. The other men carefully laid him down and started blowing their warm breath in his face and rubbing his stiff body. He slowly regained consciousness, and they could continue on their way. Arriving at a spot where reed cutters had been at work, the fugitive men decided to wait until the workers returned after Christmas and then get help from them.

While Bram was reconnoitering the area, Ben and Jurrie fell into a deep sleep. The next morning when they awoke they were numb. They understood they were suffering from hypothermia and would freeze to death if they did nothing. They warmed up their fingers with their breath and slowly started moving. There was no sign whatsoever of Bram and desperately the two of them stumbled on frostbitten feet at random into the nearest open country. It did not take long before they were spotted by the Germans, who arrested them. With his injured foot, Ben could not even manage one more step, and after the Germans slapped and kicked him a few times, they dragged him off. He and Jurrie were taken to a post and to a lieutenant who had been in charge of the search. Some fifteen minutes later, Bram was also brought in.

This put an end to the search by the Germans as almost all fugitives, including the Allied pilots, had been arrested. Only two men had managed to reach Canadian lines. The German lieutenant's task was done and he was not unfriendly towards his prisoners. After all, it was still Christmas. They were given schnapps and coffee to drink and could fill their stomachs with bread and apples. Each was allowed to light an imitation cigarette. That same night they were turned over to the *Feldgendarmerie* (German police) and transferred to the office of the *Sicherheitsdienst* (SD, German intelligence service) in Strijen for questioning. The three of them feared they would be marched to the wall to be executed, but they were spared this fate, although Jurrie, in particular, was severely tortured by an SD agent during interrogation.

The threesome was transferred to SD headquarters on the Heemraadsingel in Rotterdam and from there to the local police station on the Haagsche Veer. As the men were still suffering from the effects of their frostbitten feet (Ben's had started to become infected), they succeeded in being transferred to the Zuider hospital for treatment. There they were liberated by armed resistance fighters who overpowered their guards and transferred the three men to hiding places in town. All three survived the war.

From 1969 until his death in 1980, Ben Beukema was mayor of 's Gravenmoer in Brabant.[26] His story about the events in the Christmas period of 1944, was published on December 25, 1946, in *De Zwerver* (The Wanderer), the periodical of the *Landelijke Organisatie voor Hulp aan Onderduikers* (LO, national organization to assist persons in hiding) and the *Landelijke Knokploegen* (KP, the national resistance fighting units). Not all of those participating in this fateful attempt to reach the liberated south were as lucky as the threesome above. One was shot by the Germans while being transferred from the Oranjehotel (German prison in Scheveningen) to Camp Amersfoort. On January 7, 1945, another four were executed by a firing squad in Bergschenhoek near Rotterdam. Their deaths, along with six others, were in reprisal for the shooting of one German soldier by a Dutch young man.[27] Christmas 1944 had been their last.

The relentless actions by the occupier against the resistance had become daily routine in 1944. In addition, in that year many men had been drafted for labor in Germany in connection with the *Ar-*

beitseinsatz (forced labor deployment). In particular though, it was the famine above all during the winter of 1944/1945 that caused much suffering. This was the result of the order by *Reichskommissar* (state commissioner) Arthur Seyss-Inquart to halt all inland shipping. His order was a reprisal against the general railway strike which had been ordered by the Dutch government on September 17, 1944, in support of Operation Market Garden and with which the Dutch complied on a large scale. As a result of Seyss-Inquart's order, the densely populated western part of the country (the Randstad, which included Amsterdam, Rotterdam, The Hague, and Utrecht) was cut off from food and fuel.

After the lifting of the blockade six weeks later, inland shipping was resumed with great difficulty. When canals and rivers as well as the IJsselmeer froze over in December, ship traffic was impossible until February. For the population in the Randstad, the consequences were severe. City-dwellers went en masse to the countryside to obtain food. In order to warm themselves in the harsh winter, people even used furniture as fuel. Owing to the scarce and unvaried foods on the one hand and the deteriorating hygienic situation on the other, conditions like hunger edema, tuberculosis and scabies erupted. Dysentery and diphtheria were rampant among children. No less than 200,000 people had to be treated in hospital for malnutrition. During the winter famine, an estimated 20,000 to 22,000 people died of inadequate nutrition, sickness and exhaustion.[28]

Dark, cold, and shortages – these words describe the Christmas celebration of many residents of the major cities in the west. In their apartment over Café De IJsbreker along the Amstel in Amsterdam, the Crone couple spent the Christmas holidays for the most part in bed as this was the only place in the house where it was warm. Fuel for the stove was barely available. When they got out of bed, they walked around in coats and hats. Light was provided by a few candles and a kerosene lantern as there was no electricity either. Likewise, food was scarce, and their Christmas dinner consisted of only winter carrots and nothing else. They had bought a little Christmas tree though. The couple still had some flour and butter in the house, but they had agreed to save it until New Year's Eve to bake some Dutch pancakes, which they did using a few pieces of wood and a make-shift stove.

For the Amsberg family, also living in Amsterdam, at Christmas there was little more than the smell of pancakes being baked by the neighbors across the street. The Amsbergs had hardly anything to eat themselves. Their daughter Kiki, four years of age at the time, could only recall after the war that she had shared a tin of sweetened condensed milk among the three of them as a Christmas dinner. She had lost her cat as well. According to her parents, the animal had been stolen. It's very possible that her cat was not the only one that disappeared into some starving family's cooking pot.[29]

In Scheveningen near The Hague, the Christmas atmosphere was hardly any better than in the capital. According to the fisherman Cor van Toorn, hardly anyone enjoyed Christmas. Without heating and by the light of a lone candle, after around 19:00 or 19:30 there was little else to do but go to bed. He knew it was December 25 but that was all there was to it. Since September, he was employed in the soup kitchen on the Van Alkemadelaan where food supplies had decreased considerably. In September, 20 packs of butter were added to the soup pots of 135 gallons; in December this had dropped to just one. With 10 crates of salad added, this mixture had to pass for vegetable soup.

Two days before Christmas he and a few others were dispatched with horse and carriage to get potatoes from the cellar of a government building on the Oostduinlaan. The whole floor was covered with them but most were rotten. Nevertheless, everything was taken. Then the good potatoes were selected and thrown into the peeling machine. These peeled potatoes were distributed as a supplement on the two Christmas days (in the Netherlands Christmas is celebrated on 25 and 26 December). Another addition to the Christmas ration was a small bowl of mashed potatoes and cabbage with a little bacon for everyone. The people who received this food, according to Cor, found this Christmas addition marvelous, but after Christmas they would have to make do again with gradually dwindling rations.[30]

In the home of Catholic politician P.J.M. Aalberse in The Hague, "only one room could be moderately heated and only for a few hours per day" in the period prior to Christmas because of the shortage of coal. He wondered if they could make it until Christmas with the dwindling coal supply. He wrote: "Sitting in the cold all the time with numb fingers and icy feet was even worse than being hungry." Many of his fellow citizens set off to gather wood to fuel their stoves. Every day he saw upper-class as well as lower-class people "carrying bundles of branches they had collected in the bushes. Often, entire trees were cut down." According to Aalberse, it was impossible to heat the house above 10°C on the Christmas holidays. There was no electricity either, and the only source of light in the Aalberse home was a few candles which had to be used sparingly, causing the family to sit in the dark at night for a long time. A good night's rest was a rarity as well because V-1s and V-2s were launched not far from the city, causing a lot of noise.

The news of the German breakthrough in the Ardennes had also reached the Netherlands, adding to the dejected mood of the Christmas days. "The hope of being finally liberated after five long years has been pushed back into the far distance again," Aalberse wrote in his diary. "Added to this was the dire situation in which we lived .... Potatoes, our main source of food, are now rationed to 1 kilo per person per week. The bread ration had already been reduced to 1500 grams per week. Vegetables have not been available for weeks. That is what we were facing. Each night, we went to bed hungry."

The food situation in the northern and eastern parts of the Netherlands was less dire than elsewhere because in those parts, farmers provided an acceptable supply of food. Unlike starving residents in the Randstad, the Aalberse family did not need to search for food in the holiday period the Aalberse family did not need to search for food in the holiday period as it was simply delivered to them. Friends from Zevenaar had sent them a large parcel that was delivered the Friday before Christmas. "So many delicious things in there," Aalberse enthusiastically entered in his diary. "A beautiful chunk of pork, three hard-boiled eggs, many legumes, powdered milk and so on and on. Yes, even an extravagant luxury for me, a bag of delicious pre-war tobacco!" He and his mother got tears in their eyes and danced around the table in enjoyment. After Christmas they received some more legumes and "two delicious mutton chops" from other friends outside The Hague. "So at Christmas we felt like kings," according to the author, and "we did not have to lie in bed yawning with an empty stomach."[31]

The Christmas editions of the *De Telegraaf* (a pro-German Dutch newspaper) may have sounded cheerful and hopeful in the previous years, but in 1944 the editors could not ignore the sad reality. Because of the rationing, the paper was thinner, and instead of publishing light and humorous articles, pictures and ads, it now contained news about rationing, profiteers and the war. Although the front page of the December 23 issue was decorated with holly, the headlines of "Somber Christmas 1944", "Heavy attacks on German flanks" and "German leading units advancing further west" told their own story. A Christmas crossword puzzle and the children's corner had not been omitted, however.

"No smell of fir branches, no glistening candles, no festively laid table," the somber editorial comment started, "everything which used to make Christmas sparkling and delightful ... has slipped away from us." Not a word was said about Nazism and its leader but the suggestion was made to find support from belief in Jesus in an article entitled "The Child." "Can these silent days ask a small return favor of us," the article asked, "the favor of commemorating with the entire fondness of our soul all men, fathers and brothers who have been deported along strange roads, the injured in all hospitals whose tears are burning in their eyes because their dearest wish has passed, the blackened cities and the wounded earth, even if the nerves of our hearts are writhing with pain when we do so?"[32]

On December 22, 1944, *De Telegraaf* reported that the flower and Christmas tree market on the Singel in Amsterdam, "where around this time in other years, a penetrating fragrance of fir was in the air, showed a somber picture this year." Large Christmas trees were nowhere in sight, but small ones and fir branches were for sale. There was a lively trade in Christmas greens "as there are still many wishing to decorate their room with a simple Christmas branch." Elsewhere in the city, the sale of Christmas trees was prohibited. In the windows of flower shops beautiful bouquets, even with tall white candles, were on display but were sold at "fantastic prices." According to the reporter, there was not much else to see of Christmas in the shops in the capital. Christmas pastry rings, Christmas stollen and other luxuries were not for sale at all because all confectioner's shops had been "closed hermetically for months."[33]

The next day, the same paper reported that many traders in Christmas greens had raised their prices considerably, because, in their words, the purchase price was also high. "The Amsterdammers who wanted to buy green Christmas branches, red holly or white cyclamen on the flower market on the Singel or in shops, soon came to the conclusion that the prices only had one color: black." The Prijsbeheersing (price control agency) had taken action against "51 shops, including large stores and stalls." Prices were lowered under pressure, and at the flower market "immediately long lines formed of eager buyers who could now buy greens or flowers at set prices."[34]

The underground press also paid special attention to Christmas. In *Het Nieuws*, published in The Hague from June 1944 until March

1945, a symbolic article was published on December 24, 1944, about a 20-year-old resistance fighter who refused to betray his friends to the occupier and who consequently died for his country. The similarity with that other figure of simple origins who sacrificed himself for humanity cannot have been a coincidence during the Christmas days. "His spirit lives on within us, his friends," the resistance paper read. "He is now our shining example. He did not speak, and it cost him his life, which he sacrificed for us." The editorial ended with words to the resistance fighter. "Full of hope, you were looking forward to Christmas and to the liberation of your and our homeland. May you have the liberation and peace that the world cannot give, and may it be the beginning of an eternal, happy, peaceful Christmas. That will be our prayer for you." On the back page of the paper was a drawing of a man looking out the window at a little church with four Allied aircraft flying over it. "Christmas 1944, liberation is near," the hopeful caption reads.[35]

The front page of the December 21, 1944, Haarlem edition of the Christian resistance paper *Trouw* (Loyalty) depicted a drawing of baby Jesus in the Christmas stable. Above him is an angel with a sword, flanked by the ominous figures of Death and a German soldier. A frightening claw, the symbol of hunger, stretches toward the child in the manger. "Peace wins," the accompanying text reads. "The power of peace of Jesus Christ, the Son of God, will finally put everything in place – and the war and the hunger and all suffering shall give way. Light is shining in the darkness."[36]

Illustration from the resistance paper Het Nieuws (The News) of December 24, 1944. (Delpher)

The front page of the Haarlem edition of the Christian resistance paper Trouw (Loyalty) of December 21st 1944. (Delpher)

Notes chapter VI:

[1] English, E., Letter to his mother, 25 Dec. 1944, www.shak1944.org.
[2] E-mail from Mr. Jons van Dooren, chairman of SHAK44, 11 Mar. 2018.
[3] English, E., Letter to his mother, 25 December 1944, www.shak1944.org.
[4] Bartholomeus, V., 'Ondergronds kerstfeest', *Limburgs Dagblad*, 22 Dec. 2012.
[5] E-mail from Mr. Jons van Dooren, chairman of SHAK44, 11 Mar. 2018; Anoniem, ooggetuigenverslag Amerikaanse kerstviering 24 Dec. 1944, SHAK.
[6] Budzyna, T., 'Relive Christmas 1944 in special De Schark Cave service', website U.S. Army, 12 Dec. 2011.
[7] Kok, R. & Somers, E., *Nederland en de Tweede Wereldoorlog*, pp. 346, 350, 355.
[8] Jansen, C., *Mijn dagboek van de oorlogsjaren 1940 – 1945*, p. 65.
[9] Sjenitzer-van Leening, T.M., *Dagboekfragmenten 1940-1945*, p. 483.
[10] VPRO-radio Het Spoor Terug, 'Kerst 1944', 27 Dec. 1987.
[11] '"The Little Coat," a Hand-Made Gift of Love', website Veterans Affairs Canada.
[12] NOVA, 'Suzy: de mascotte van een Canadese tankbemanning', 04 Mai 2010.
[13] NOVA, 'Suzy: de mascotte van een Canadese tankbemanning', 04 Mai 2010.
[14] 'Famous Elliots: Bob Elliott', website Elliot Clan Society.
[15] NOVA, 'Suzy: de mascotte van een Canadese tankbemanning', 04 Mai 2010.
[16] '"The Little Coat," a Hand-Made Gift of Love', website Veterans Affairs Canada.
[17] '"The Little Coat," a Hand-Made Gift of Love', website Veterans Affairs Canada; NOVA, 'Suzy: de mascotte van een Canadese tankbemanning', 04 Mai 2010.
[18] 'Famous Elliots: Bob Elliott', website Elliot Clan Society.
[19] NOVA, 'Suzy: de mascotte van een Canadese tankbemanning', 04 Mai 2010.
[20] 'Famous Elliots: Bob Elliott', website Elliot Clan Society; '"The Little Coat," a Hand-Made Gift of Love', website Veterans Affairs Canada.
[21] Website Canadian War Museum.
[22] Dankers-Van Beek, T., 'dagboek van september 1944 tot de bevrijding', TracesOfWar.nl.
[23] VPRO-radio Het Spoor Terug, 'Kerst 1944', 27 Dec. 1987.
[24] VPRO-radio Het Spoor Terug, 'Kerst 1944', 27 Dec. 1987; Sjenitzer-van Leening, T.M., *Dagboekfragmenten 1940-1945*, pp. 477-478.
[25] VPRO-radio Het Spoor Terug, 'Kerst 1944', 27 Dec. 1987.

[26] 'Kerstnacht in de griend', De Zwerver, 25 Dec. 1946; www. www.wo2-hoekschewaard.nl; Veld, C. in 't, *Het verzet in de Tweede Wereldoorlog*, pp. 48-58

[27] Veld, C. in 't, *Het verzet in de Tweede Wereldoorlog*, pp. 58-63

[28] Kok, R. & Somers, E., *Nederland en de Tweede Wereldoorlog*, pp. 427-429.

[29] VPRO-radio Het Spoor Terug, 'Kerst 1944', 27 Dec. 1987.

[30] VPRO-radio Het Spoor Terug, 'Kerst 1944', 27 Dec. 1987.

[31] Aalberse, P.J.M., *Dagboek XI: Begin november 1944 tot 7 augustus 1946*, Huygens ING digitaal archief.

[32] 'Donkere Kerstmis 1944', *De Telegraaf*, 23 Dec. 1944.

[33] 'Meer kersttakken dan boomen', *De Telegraaf*, 22 Dec. 1944

[34] 'Te dure bloemen en boomen', *De Telegraaf*, 23 Dec. 1944

[35] 'Kerstfeest 1944', *Het nieuws*, 24 Dec. 1944.

[36] 'Vrede op aarde', *Trouw : speciale uitgave Haarlem en omstreken*, 21 Dec. 1944.

- VII -
Silent Night

As an American GI looked out through the window of a freight train car in the evening of December 23, he saw a Christmas tree. Red, purple, orange and yellow lights shone brightly in the dark sky. With a little imagination these lights looked like a gigantic Christmas tree, but in reality they were marker flares that were dropped by Allied aircraft to mark the targets for the bombers. Even German citizens often compared this spectacular scene to a lighted Christmas tree.

The American – Phil Hannon of the 81st Combat Engineers – had been taken prisoner by the Germans during the Ardennes offensive and was being transported by train, along with many fellow prisoners, to a POW camp almost 40 miles east of Frankfurt. On the way they received little to eat or drink. A thin layer of straw on the floor of the freight car was the only luxury granted to them. During the journey, dysentery had broken out, and the men were forced to relieve themselves using their helmets and then throw the contents out the window. The colored lights in the sky heralded an even bigger disaster. While the prisoners took shelter in a ditch next to the railway line, the Allied bombs came down all around them. The bombs claimed eight dead and thirty-six injured. At the end the men had to return to their freight cars. The next day, Christmas Eve, they were given a slice of bread and jam that proved too much for stomachs that had been empty for days. On Christmas Day, their train rolled into Germany.[1]

Christmas time was not that austere for all Americans who were imprisoned in Germany this Christmas. In Stalag Luft III, in Sagan in Lower Silesia (which would be known after the war mainly for the great escape that took place there in March 1944), the prisoners skated on the pond on and after Christmas while music was played through loudspeakers. There also was another kind of ice. Australian pilot Syd Wickham remembers how he and his mates blended a thick mixture of powdered milk and water with a little sugar in their water jug. They put it outside the window of their barracks at night and after it had frozen they took turns beating it to aerate it. After the mixture had been outside for an another night, they could enjoy home-made ice cream.[2]

The Americans who were being nursed in a German military hospital in Attendorn near Düsseldorf did not have a bad Christmas either. On Christmas Eve at 23:00, those able to walk were invited by a nurse to join the Christmas celebration. Private Bernard Macay was one of those invited. Actually, he was afraid he and the other injured men would be put on display, because during the day German officers had taken their wives and girlfriends to the wards to shudder at the most severe injuries. But Macay had no need to worry as the Germans showed their genuine warmth. They asked the Americans to sing "Silent Night" and sang this Christmas carol themselves in German. Later on, more carols were sung in German and English. Before the prisoners returned to their wards, to their surprise they were even given a dessert.[3]

Western prisoners in German POW camps had the good fortune that, in addition to letters, they were allowed to receive parcels with food and other useful items from their homelands. Apart from their families, they also received parcels from organizations like the Red Cross and the YMCA. Prior to Christmas, these were eagerly anticipated. In the summer, the American Red Cross had already sent 75,000 Christmas parcels to ensure they would be delivered to the camps in time for Christmas.[4] An American 2nd Lieutenant in Stalag Luft I in northern Germany on the Baltic Coast summed up the contents of the parcel in a letter home. Tinned food constituted the majority: turkey, honey, butter, cheese, cooked ham, Viennese sausages, cherries, jam, nuts, candy and Christmas pudding. Furthermore, it contained a pack of dates, a package of tea, a box of beef cubes, two fruit bars, a facecloth, a pipe with a package of tobacco, three packs of cigarettes, four packs of chewing gum, and a set of playing cards. The American wrote that he and his mates had "a delicious meal" and that the deck of cards was very welcome because card games were a popular pastime in his camp.[5]

This year, not everyone was equally happy with the generous Red Cross parcel. It was all very rich in comparison to what the men were used to, and it was too much for their stomachs. An Australian in Stalag Luft III complained about the parcel which was, in his opinion, both "too luxurious" and inadequate. Instead of the tinned turkey, pudding, candy and "a lot of junk," he would have preferred milk, sugar and cookies.[6]

Other Western POWs managed to compose creative Christmas meals, with, for instance, the contents of the Red Cross Christmas parcels. In the overcrowded room in the Stalag Luft III barracks of Australian Bruce Lumsden, the prisoners – seven British, five Americans, a South-African, a Canadian, a New Zealander and three Australians – started early with their preparations. The old hands had been busy for months, setting aside foodstuffs from their Red Cross parcels. New arrival Lumsden had crashed in the Netherlands in November 1944 with his Lancaster, in which he served as navigator. He was captured but had not been imprisoned long enough to have collected anything of note. The rations the Germans provided were too small to set aside much. He was the cook in his barracks, and he doubted whether he could prepare an acceptable Christmas dinner. By cutting thinner slices of bread and spreading margarine in a thinner layer, he and his mates tried to collect something. In addition, their quartermaster took all of the most delicious items out of the parcels and kept them separate. The best chances lay in the Red Cross parcels, which arrived in time for Christmas, and the unexpected distribution of syrup and oat meal.

Lumsden set about diligently preparing a traditional Christmas meal for his mates. For the Christmas pudding, he made a dough of crusts of bread, a chocolate bar, semolina, crumbled American cookies, raisins, prunes, sugar, molasses, margarine, powdered milk, four cups of pre-cooked barley, a tin of orange juice, a spoonful of coffee and a pinch of salt. Then, each man was allowed to stir the mixture and make a wish. They did not say it aloud, but according to Lumsden it was not hard to guess they had all wished the same thing. After the mixture had been boiled for four hours and rested for a day, the pudding was finished. The Australian, who had no previous experience whatsoever as cook or baker, also made a Christmas cake which smelled delicious when it was taken from the oven of their wood-fired stove.

To make their Christmas celebration complete, in their room the men hung garlands of toilet paper which they had decorated with colored crayons. Two of Lumsden's artistic countrymen made a menu chart for each table. Before they started their Christmas dinner, devout Lumsden said a prayer which was appreciated by the others, even though some did not share the same faith and others were not religious at all. "I cannot remember the words I used in my grace," the Australian stated after the war, "but I recall the quiet participation of every man present, especially when I expressed our thoughts for our homes and families and for our return to them soon." The prayer and the dinner formed a bridge between the various nationalities and identities of the men and brought them closer together, almost as if they were a family in peacetime celebrating Christmas at home around the Christmas tree.[7]

For the holiday season, Christmas concerts and religious services were organized for the Western Allies in German POW camps. In some cases, German guards distributed little Christmas trees which could then be dressed up by the prisoners with decorations made from waste materials. Listening to the radio together and watching movies during Christmas time made for some interruption of the boredom which plagued the prisoners most of the day.[8] To break up the boredom, 24-year-old American bomber pilot Clair Cline in Stalag Luft I carved models of B-24 aircraft from wood. He had bailed out of this type of aircraft in February 1944 after it had been hit by anti-aircraft fire over occupied Holland. On landing, he was arrested by a German soldier, and soon after he was transferred to the POW camp in northern Germany. He said it was "a dismal place." He and his fellow prisoners "slept on bunks with straw-filled burlap sacks on wooden slats" in "rough wooden barracks." Although the rations were "very meager, " thanks to the Red Cross parcels the men did not starve. "But the worst affliction was our uncertainty," Cline stated after the war." Not knowing when the war would end or what would happen (we had heard rumors of prisoners being killed) left us with a constant gnawing worry."

While he passed the time carving wood and writing letters to his wife, the other men "played bridge all day, dug escape tunnels (to no avail)" or read "tattered paperbacks." In the fall of 1944, the American had enough of his wood carving. In his own words, he cast the half-finished model aside and prayed to God, asking him "please help me find something constructive to do." Then someone suddenly started whistling the song "Red Wing," and in his mind Cline was "once again seven years old in rural Minnesota listening to a fiddler sweep out the old melody." He remembered how he as a child had been given a violin by his uncle on which he had learned to play polkas. It seemed "fantastic" to play a violin in this camp. "But finding one in this place would be impossible," he concluded. "Just then I glanced at my cast-aside model, and a thought came to me: I can make one! Why not?" With the slogan of his father on his mind – "You can make something out of nothing" – he went to work. He had already obtained a pen knife by trading tobacco with the camp guards and he could use the slats of the bunks for the body of the instrument. Glue was harder to come by until Cline discovered that the brown residue of dried carpenter's glue on the chairs could be used again. With the help of the other men, he scraped it off and subsequently "ground it to powder, mixed it with water and heated it on a stove."

For weeks on end, the violin maker worked on his instrument. He shaped wood by soaking it in water and heating it over a stove. He glued several slats together to make the neck. Each morning he "could hardly wait to get back to work." After three months the body of the instrument was finished. Cline recalled: "After having sanded the wood carefully, I varnished it with lacquer I had received from guards in exchange for cigarettes. I polished it with pumice and paraffin oil until it shone with a golden glow." By trading cigarettes with guards again, he obtained catgut to use for strings and a real bow.

When he played the finished instrument for the first time, "his heart leapt" as a "pure and resonant sound echoed through the air." His fellow inmates, however, banished him to the latrine "until I had regained my old skills." From that moment on, his mates were tremendously enthusiastic when he played songs for them. "My most memorable moment was on Christmas Eve," he stated after the war. "As my buddies brooded about home and families, I began playing 'Silent Night.' As the notes drifted through the barracks, a voice chimed in, then others." Among the English singing, another language sounded suddenly. An "elderly, white-haired guard" joined the singing in German from the shadows, "his eyes wet with tears."[9]

That was not the last performance of the instrument. Years after the war, the home-made violin of Clair Cline, who passed away in 2010 at the age of 92, was being played by various violinists in concert halls throughout the United States.[10]

Not all forms of entertainment during Christmas in German POW camps were serious, as the story of American Earl Wasson of the 466th Bomb Group proves. He was interned in Stalag Luft I in 1944 and described the camp as "Hell," because of the "unending frigid weather, the unpredictable behavior of the guards. Inadequate food, lice, sickness, boredom, death by starvation or by exposure was their unchanging agenda." It was a pleasant interruption of the monotonous camp life when a fresh contingent of POWs arrived with "unbiased running accounts of how the war was progressing on both the

Eastern Front with the Russians and on the Western Front." The news about German losses and the "increasing number of bombers and fighters appearing in the air overhead" raised optimism in 1944, according to Wasson. "Liberation was on everybody's lips," he said. "The war was indeed winding down!" There was even talk about being home for Christmas. One of the prisoners was so convinced of it he made a bet with a skeptical man. "If we aren't home by Christmas, I will kiss your a** before the whole group formation right after head-count on Christmas morning," he said self-assuredly to his opponent, and they shook hands on it. As the situation had not changed on Christmas Day, the loser had to pay his debt.

On Christmas morning an icy wind was blowing in from the sea. After all POWs had been counted on the parade ground, all men remained where they were except the two bettors, who left the formation and entered one of the barracks. "No one else moved!" according to Wasson. "The guards were puzzled. They did not know what was going on." It did not take long for the pair to return. The loser carried a bucket of soapy water and a towel to wipe the butt of the winner, who first lowered his trousers and bent over as the other prisoners looked on laughing. "The German guards and dignitaries of Barth stood gazing in amazement, they didn't know what was going on," Wasson recalled. "Then the optimist bent over and kissed his opponent on the rear! A mighty cheer went up from over 2,000 men. Then the puzzled guards joined in the fun."

After the hilarious Christmas morning, the rest of the day seemed to proceed like any other day. The "Kriegies," as the POWs often called themselves using slang for the German word *Kriegsgefangene*, received the same black bread and thin soup as on any other day. At night, Wasson and his mates were sitting together in their cold barracks. They had another long and miserable night ahead of them until the door was opened and a voice called out that curfew had been lifted and a Christmas celebration would be held in the next compound in the camp. In the bitter cold and with the new snow crunching beneath their feet, the men walked straight to the location. It was the first time they had been outdoors in the camp after sunset. Bright stars shone in the sky over their heads, and the northern lights lit up the frosty sky. After arriving in the compound where the Christmas celebration was to be held, the prisoners sang the inevitable "Silent Night" together. The German guards interrupted their rounds and joined the celebration. Although the lyrics of the song were unknown to them, they knew the melody well. They relaxed and joined in, singing in German. According to Wasson, the words of the Christmas carol penetrated the hearts of the prisoners and they felt satisfaction. "Tonight, they would sleep in peace. War and imprisonment were not powerful enough to destroy the meaning and the beauty of this special day. It was Christmas. They were not at home. But they declared, 'Next year, we will be! All of us! ' And they were!"[11]

Fraternization between western POWs and their German guards during the Christmas period was not unusual. American Wilson Elliott celebrated his 20th birthday on Christmas Day 1944 in captivity. He was made a POW on April 17, 1943, after his B-17 had been downed over Germany. Five of his crew died. On Christmas morning he dejectedly looked out the window at the scenery which consisted of barbed wire fences and "shivering German soldiers on guard." "I would have given almost anything to be at home, hovering around a hot stove or fireplace. I could almost smell Mother's cooking." The day seemed to proceed without festivities and presents. A German sergeant, a veteran from World War I, paid a visit to Elliott's barracks to wish him and his mates a Merry Christmas and to have a cup of tea. The man was not popular among the prisoners because he was the one who called them to roll call three times a day and searched their barracks for contraband.

Prior to resuming his morning rounds through the camp, he addressed Elliott. He had a more or less friendly relationship with him as he accompanied the American on his visits to other camps to play music by German composers on a record player. "Looking at me with a slight smile on his face," Elliott recalls, "the Sgt. reached into his long winter uniform coat and pulled out a bottle of wine and an apple. I hadn't seen an apple since I left the States. 'Merry Christmas and Happy Birthday,' he said as he handed me the gifts and disappeared through the door into a cold outside winter day. This was a time that I probably will remember forever."[12]

On Christmas 1944, Canadian Vince A. Calder had been a POW of the Japanese for three years. Steamed rice and hot water passing for tea were the only things he and his mates expected to receive as Christmas dinner. Their daily rations amounted to not much more. The spirit of the POWs, weakened by hunger was low. When at 11:00 a Japanese sergeant appeared in the "dining hall", the men had no idea their day would proceed differently from what was expected. The Japanese asked for fifty volunteers to carry Red Cross parcels to the camp. "Every man that could walk or crawl volunteered," according to Calder, "and although we were pretty weak and skinny, we walked 2 miles to the station and back."

This day, the Japanese had no nasty jokes up their sleeves. Calder and his fellow prisoners "couldn't believe it when we saw that there was a parcel for every man in camp." The camp commander let it be known he had kept the parcels for two weeks so they could be distributed on Christmas. When his prisoners offered him and the sergeant some candy and cigarettes in gratitude he rejected their offer, saying they needed it more badly than he did. As an extra bonus, some candy, beer and sake were distributed among the men. For Calder it had been three years since he had had alcohol and the next morning, he paid for it with a "terrible hangover." In addition the men were allowed to roam through the camp freely, and they would not be harassed by the guards provided "no one tried to escape or got drunk." They celebrated Christmas with a concert performed by an orchestra using instruments they had made themselves.[13]

Even for Jewish forced laborer Anna Ostrowiak from Warsaw, there was an unexpected treat waiting. She was interned in a labor camp in Czestochowa in Poland and was, along with other women, deployed on an airfield where they had to clear the runway of snow and ice. When they arrived at work on Christmas Day, she and her fellow inmates saw "a Christmas cake in a paper bag" which had been left on a bench near the shed where their equipment was stored. The German soldier guarding them must have seen it lying there as well, but he did nothing. Throughout the day, the women discussed the risk of taking the treat and eating it.

When later in the day, totally exhausted and hungry, they went to store their tools, the cake was still in the same spot, untouched. Their guard, who had shouted his orders at them all day, suddenly left them alone. The women were speechless until one of them broke the silence. "There is something phony about this guy," she allegedly said. "First of all, he yelled at us too much and too loud, and now he walks out and leaves us unguarded? I don't care what you do, but I am going to take a piece of that cake and eat it right now. I am not afraid of him." "Like hungry animals we all fell in line and within a minute, the cake was gone," Anna Ostrowiak recalls. Not a crumb was wasted. On the bottom of the bowl they found a note with the message: "Glory to the Highest, Peace on Earth." After their guard had returned, he escorted them back to their barracks in silence, "his gun still drawn, his boots still loudly hitting the ground."[14]

Even during Christmas, some of the concentration camp guards did not control their sadism. The guards in the Neuengamme concentration camp near Hamburg also seemed to grant their prisoners a little rest on Christmas Eve. The total number of people who perished in this camp would be at least 42,900, including political opponents, resistance fighters, Jews, Roma and Sinti Gypsies and homosexuals.[15] Dutch resistance fighter Jan van der Liet, who had been arrested in July 1944 at the age of seventeen and had been deported to Neuengamme in December, remembered the silence in the large parade ground where he and the other inmates had assembled around a Christmas tree adorned with lights. In the eyes of his fellow prisoners he saw that fear had temporarily left them. Motionless, they stared at the soft light of the bulbs while their thoughts carried them away from that hell of horror back to their loved ones. According to Van der Liet, "it was the only rest I ever experienced in a concentration camp and I let myself be carried away too; it felt so good to imagine myself being at home." He saw in his mind's eye how his mother was laying the Christmas table and lighting the candles in the Christmas tree. The melody of "Silent Night" played on a violin by an Hungarian Jew brought them back to reality. Thousands of men joined in singing the song and all "forgot their suffering and imagined they were happy. "

The moment was cut short. Suddenly pistol shots rang out and aggressive barking was heard. The laughing guards had unleashed their dogs, and the inmates fled to their barracks in panic. "The elderly stumbled," said the Dutchman "and were trampled to death by thousands of feet. Those in the rear were being attacked by dogs biting like savages and tearing the clothes off bodies." Van der Liet managed to reach his barracks safely and jumped straight into bed. Just when it had become quiet, the guards resumed their sadistic game. They made all inmates leave their barracks and stand in line for roll call in the cold. After 90 minutes they were allowed back in only to receive the order soon after to stand in line again. It wasn't until 04:00 in the morning that everyone could finally go to sleep. When suddenly the violinist resumed playing, all the inmates in Van der Liet's barracks got out of bed to listen. "When the fingers of the musician grew too stiff to continue playing, they all started singing.

Everyone sang in his own language and everyone prayed in his own language for salvation and liberation from this hell on earth."[16]

In the Bavarian camp of Flossenbürg, Christmas was not peaceful either. Six Russian POWs had not succeeded in their attempt to escape. When the other prisoners returned from work on Christmas night, they were taken to witness the hanging of the six from a gallows specially built next to a large Christmas tree. Jakub Sztabmacher, a teenage prisoner who had lost his parents and siblings in the Holocaust, later reported that an "SS man walked down the ranks and looked us right in the face to see if we showed some kind of compassion, but we had learned to make our faces freeze into a mask." Sadly, that image of the gallows lit by the beautiful tree was one of the most vivid from Flossenburg for many because, explained one witness, Milos Volf, "a Christmas tree is a symbol of love and peace."[17] The cruel tragedy has been described in words and art by former inmates, including the Austrian Hugo Walleitner.[18]

Christmas Eve 1944 in Flossenbürg.
Untitled drawing by camp inmate Hugo Walleitner.
(Flossenbürg Concentration Camp Memorial)

Notes chapter VII:

[1] Astor, G., *A Blood-Dimmed Tide*, pp. 292-293.

[2] Alexander, K., 'So another Kriegie Xmas passes': Christmas in Stalag Luft III, weblog Australians in Stalag Luft III.

[3] Neill, G.W., *Infantry Soldier: Holding the Lines at the Battle of the Bulge*, pp. 270-271.

[4] Guise, K., 'Kriegie Christmas, 1944', website The National WWII Museum New Orleans.

[5] 'World War II - Prisoners of War - Stalag Luft I', www.merkki.com.

[6] Alexander, K., 'So another Kriegie Xmas passes': Christmas in Stalag Luft III, weblog Australians in Stalag Luft III.

[7] Alexander, K., 'So another Kriegie Xmas passes': Christmas in Stalag Luft III, weblog Australians in Stalag Luft III.

[8] Guise, K., 'Kriegie Christmas, 1944', website The National WWII Museum New Orleans.

[9] Cline, C., 'The Prison Camp Violin Clair Cline and the prison camp violin - Stalag Luft I', *Guidepost Magazine*, Jan. 1997, www.merkki.com/violin.htm.

[10] Catlin, R., 'National Symphony Orchestra violist plays heirloom built by grandfather', *The Washington Post*, 29 Mai 2015.

[11] Wasson, E., 'The Bet at Barth', www.merkki.com/barthbet.htm.

[12] Elliott, W., 'Christmas during WWII', website American Ex-Prisoners of War.

[13] 'Rifleman Vince A. Calder - Hong Kong POW', Hong Kong Veterans Commemorative Association.

[14] Gilbert, M., *The Righteous*, pp. 499-500.

[15] Website KZ-Gedenkstätte Neuengamme.

[16] Schuyf, J., *Nederlanders in Neuengamme*, pp. 159-160.

[17] Knopp, G., Als die Welt einen Moment innehielt: "Der Tod von Flossenbürg." *Welt am Sonntag*. 19 Dec. 2004, www.welt.de/print-wams/article119499/Als-die-Welt-einen-Moment-innehielt.html.

[18] E-mail from Annabelle Lienhart KZ-Gedenkstätte Flossenbürg, 14 Dec. 2017.

Conclusion

"Six years of misery, terror and destruction have not killed Santa Claus." That was the conclusion of journalist Anne O'Hare McCormick in an article on Christmas in Europe for the *New York Times* of December 25, 1945. While Europeans attempted to resume their normal lives and had started on the first reconstruction projects, the American woman saw an "eagerness of people this year to hold on to Christmas."[1] In the dark war years that had passed, Christmas had never disappeared, neither in Europe nor in the United States nor in countries where Allied military were fighting for freedom. Of course there were those who had been distracted too much or whose suffering was too severe to celebrate Christmas, but even people who had been tested to the ultimate displayed a notably strong will to honor Christmas, however rare or desperate the situations might have been in which they found themselves.

In the dark years of need, privation and suffering, Christmas could be a shining beacon. The Christmas message of peace and brotherhood among nations seemed to have been shoved aside, but it actually was more relevant than in peacetime. The Christmas days were a time on which the yearning for peace was expressed. Letters and presents from home gave military personnel at the front or in captivity not only a view of the life they had left behind but also what was on the horizon once the weapons were laid down. The senselessness of war was evident in Europe where fighting raged between opponents who sang the same Christmas carols but in another language. At the same time, celebrating Christmas was a motivation to keep on fighting. German soldiers were called on by Joseph Goebbels not to give up the fight against the Bolshevist enemy whose aim it was to eradicate the Christian celebration of Christmas. Allied soldiers in their turn were ordered to fight the enemy in order to bring closer the Christmas promise of peace on earth.

Today, thoughts of the sacrifices and horror of the past in the Christmas period are far away. In the modern Christmas celebration, contemplation has been replaced by cheerfulness. During our Christmas dinners, few of us think of the American soldiers who fought for freedom in the icy Ardennes forests on Christmas 1944. Few of us remember the many Dutch people who, with empty stomachs, went to bed early to keep warm during the winter famine. When we sit down in the glow of the Christmas tree lights and enjoy all the food and drinks that were purchased in well-stocked supermarkets without ration cards, few of us realize that during the war years places at the Christmas dinner table were empty and sometimes would remain empty forever. Celebrating Christmas in peace and abundance is a matter of course for many. The stories told in this book can be important to understanding the essence of a prosperous, peacetime Christmas. Blood was spilled for the way we in the western world celebrate Christmas today – without interference by the government, without shortages and rationing, without the massive absence of next of kin, and without fear.

[1] Litt, M., *Christmas 1945*, p. 75.

Sources

BOOKS:

- *A Century of Christmas Memories, 1900-1999*, Peter Pauper Press, New York, 2009.
- Abrams, J. & Felsenburg Marx, E., Tenuous Threads / One of the Lucky Ones, Azrieli Foundation, Toronto, 2012.
- Ambrose, S.E., *Citizen Soldiers*, Premier Digital Publishing, 2011.
- Anderson, C.E., *Keep Your Ducks in a Row! – Keep Your Ducks in a Row! The Manhattan Project Hanford, Washington 1943-1945*, Page Publishing, New York, 2016.
- Axelrod, A., *Patton: A Biography*, St. Martin's Griffin, New York, 2009.
- Ballhausen, H., *Chronik des Zweiten Weltkriegs*, Chronik Verlag, München, 2004.
- Baraitre, I., *Patton: Een Generaal in de Ardennen*, Lannoo, Tielt, 2006.
- Barron, L. & Cygan, D., *No Silent Night: The Christmas Battle For Bastogne*, Penguin Publishing Group, London, 2012.
- Beevor, A., *De Tweede Wereldoorlog*, Ambo, Amsterdam, 2012.
- Beevor, A., *Het Ardennenoffensief*, Ambo Anthos, Amsterdam, 2015.
- Berger, F., *Finding Foxholes*, North Star Press, St Cloud (Minnesota, US), 2014.
- Bornemann, J. e.a., *Zwischen Franken und der Front – Weihnachten in Kriegszeiten*, Echter Verlag, Würzburg, 2014.
- Brandt, N., *Harlem at War: The Black Experience in WWII*, Syracuse University Press, New York, 1996.
- Brown, M, *Christmas on the Home Front*, The History Press, Stroud (Gloucestershire), 2013.
- Brown, M., *A Wartime Christmas 1939-1945*, Pitkin Publishing, 2012.
- Cooper, A. & Beevor, A., *Paris After the Liberation: 1944 – 1949*, Penguin Publishing Group, London, 2004.

- Corsi, J., *No Greater Valor: The Siege of Bastogne and the Miracle That Sealed Allied Victory*, Nelson Books, Nashville (Tennessee, US), 2014.
- Cowper, W., *The Words of War: British Forces' Personal Letters and Diaries During the Second World War*, Mainstream Publishing, Edinburgh, 2009.
- Cronkite IV, W. & Isserman, M., *Cronkite's War: His World War II Letters Home*, National Geographic Society, Washington, 2013.
- Delaforce, P., *The Battle of the Bulge: Hitler's Final Gamble*, Pen & Sword, Barnsley, 2014.
- Dietrich, M., *Marlene*, Open Road, New York, 2012.
- Farris, J., *A Soldier's Sketchbook*, National Geographic Society, 2011.
- Gantter, R., *Roll Me Over: An Infantryman's World War II*, Presidio Press, Novato (Californië, US) 1997.
- Gilbert, M., *The Righteous – The unsung heroes of the Holocaust*, Black Swan, London, 2003.
- Grier, D., *Hitler, Donitz, and the Baltic Sea: The Third Reich's Last Hope, 1944-1945*, Naval Institute Press, Annapolis (Maryland, US), 2013.
- Himmler, K. & Wildt. M., *Heinrich Himmler privé – Brieven aan zijn vrouw 1927-1945*, Atlas Contact, Amsterdam 2014.
- Holmes, R., *40-45 Van Blitzkrieg tot Hiroshima*, Lannoo, Tielt, 2015.
- Hunt, I.A., *Op schoot bij Hitler – Een jeugd in een paradijs dat geen paradijs mocht zijn*, Bert Bakker, Amsterdam, 2005.
- Kellerhoff, S.F., *Berlin im Krieg: Eine Generation erinnert sich*, Bastei Lübbe, Keulen, 2011.
- Kelly, C.C., *Manhattan Project: The Birth of the Atomic Bomb in the Words of Its Creators*, Black Dog & Leventhal, New York, 2009.
- Kelly, C.C., *Remembering the Manhattan Project: Perspectives on the Making of the Atomic Bomb and its Legacy*, World Scientific Publishing Co., Signapore, 2005.
- Kershaw, A. *The Longest Winter: The Epic Story of World War II's Most Decorated Platoon*, Penguin Publishing, 2015.
- Kok, R. & Somers, E., *Nederland En De Tweede Wereldoorlog*, Waanders, Zwolle, 2005.

- König, W. von, *Wolfhilde's Hitler Youth Diary 1939-1946*, Iuniverse, Indiana, 2013.
- Liese, H., *Deutsche Kriegsweihnacht*, Hauptkulturamt der NSDAP, Berlin, 1944.
- Litt, M., *Christmas 1945 – The Story of the Greatest Celebration in American History*, History Publishing Company, New York, 2010.
- Longerich, P., *Heinrich Himmler – Hitlers belangrijkste handlanger*, De Bezige Bij, Amsterdam, 2008.
- Masuda, H., *MacArthur in Asia: The General and His Staff in the Philippines, Japan, and Korea*, Cornell University Press, Ithaca (US), 2012.
- Mitcham, S.W. jr., *The German Defeat in the East, 1944-45*, Stackpole Books, Mechanicsburg (Pennsylvania, US) 2007.
- Moore, C.P., *Fighting for America*, Presidio Press, New York, 2006.
- Nalty, B., *The Right to Fight: African-American Marines in World War II*, CreateSpace,1995.
- Neill, G.W., *Infantry Soldier: Holding the Lines at the Battle of the Bulge*, University of Oklahoma Press, Norman (Oklahoma, US), 2002.
- Patton, G., *War As I Knew It*, Houghton Mifflin, Boston/New York, 1995.
- Perry, J., *Christmas in Germany – A Cultural History*, University of North Carolina Press, Chapel Hill, 2010.
- Pitt, B, *Churchill and the Generals*, Pen and Sword, Barnsley (GB), 2004.
- Ring, J., *Storming the Eagle's Nest: Hitler's War in the Alps*, Faber & Faber, London, 2013.
- Rogers, D. & Williams, S.R., *On the Bloody Road to Berlin: Frontline Accounts from North-West Europe and the Eastern Front, 1944-1945*, Helion Company, Solihull (GB), 2005.
- Roosevelt, E., *My Day*, Da Capo Press, Da Capo Press, Cambridge (Massachusetts), 2009.
- Rosen, J., *White Christmas – The Story of an American Song*, Scribner, New York, 2002.
- Rozett, R. & Spector, S., *Encyclopedie van de Holocaust*, Kok, Kampen, 2004.
- Said, E. & Hitchens, C. (reds.), *Blaming the Victims: Spurious Scholarship and the Palestinian Question*, Verso, New York, 2001.

- Sarkar, D., *The Sinking of HMS Royal Oak: In the Words of the Survivors*, Amberley Publishing Limited, Gloucestershire, 2012.
- Schrijvers, P., *The Unknown Dead: Civilians in the Battle of the Bulge*, University Press of Kentucky, Lexington (Kentucky, US), 2005.
- Schrijvers, P., *Those Who Hold Bastogne*, Yale University Press, New Haven/London, 2014.
- Schuyf, J. (red.), *Nederlanders in Neuengamme*, Aprilis, Zaltbommel, 2005.
- Short, N., *The Führer's Headquarters: Hitler's command bunkers 1939–45*, Osprey Publishing, Oxford (GB), 2010.
- Sjenitzer-van Leening, T.M., *Dagboekfragmenten 1940-1945*, Nijhoff, den Haag, 1954.
- Spragg, D.M., Glenn Miller Declassified, Potomac Books, Lincoln (Nebraska, US), 2017.
- Taylor, J.E., *Freedom to Serve: Truman, Civil Rights, and Executive Order 9981*, Routledge, New York, 2013.
- The Library of Congress, *I'll be Home for Christmas – The Spirit of Christmas During World War II*, Gramercy Books, New York, 2006.
- Thompson, J., *De bevrijding*, Kosmos Z&K, Utrecht, 2005.
- Toland, J., *Battle: The Story of the Bulge*, Bison Books, Lincoln, Nebraska, 1999.
- Ungváry, K., *Battle for Budapest: 100 Days in World War II*, I.B. Tauris, London, 2011.
- Veld, C. in 't, *Het verzet in de Tweede Wereldoorlog*, Het land van Strijen, Strijen, 2015.
- Vogt, H.R., *My Memories of Berlin: A Young Boy's Amazing Survival Story*, Xlibris, Bloomington (Indiana, US), 2008.
- Waggoner, S., *Christmas Memories – Gifts, activities, fads, and fancies*, 1920s-1960s, Abrams, New York, 2009.
- Weintraub, S., *11 Days in December – Christmas at the Bulge, 1944*, NAL Caliber, New York, 2007.
- White, W.F., *A Man Called White: The Autobiography of Walter White*, University of Georgia Press, Athens (Georgia, US), 1995.
- Winterberg, S. & Winterberg, Y., *Kriegskinder: Erinnerungen einer Generation*, Rotbuch Verlag, Berlin, 2013.

- Womer, J. & DeVito, S.C., *Fighting with the Filthy Thirteen*, Casemate Publishers, Havertown (Pennsylvania, US), 2012.

ARTICLES:

- 'Minn. Church Recalls How Christmas Carols Saved Some U.S. Lives in World War II', *PBS Newshour*, 23 Dec. 2011.
- Ast, W.F., 'Seeing the war through the eyes of a Hitler Youth', *The Herald Palladium*, 28 Feb. 2013;
- Bartholomeus, V., 'Ondergronds kerstfeest', *Limburgs Dagblad*, 22 Dec. 2012.
- Beevor, A., 'The Christmas Day the snow turned red', *The Daily Mail*, 24 Dec. 2015.
- Beilue, J.M., 'World War II soldier brought American Christmas to French child', *Amarillo Globe-News*, 20 Jul. 206.
- Budzyna, T., 'Relive Christmas 1944 in special De Schark Cave service', *website U.S. Army*, 12 Dec. 2011.
- Burger, T.W., 'Christmas under the Gun', *America in WWII*, Dec. 2005.
- Catlin, R., 'National Symphony Orchestra violist plays heirloom built by grandfather', *The Washington Post*, 29 Mai 2015.
- Engelke, J., 'Wie die Berliner in den dunkelsten Stunden feierten, Kriegsweihnacht 1944', *B.Z. Berlin*, 19 Dec. 2004.
- Felchner, W.J., 'Collectible World War II Christmas Cards', *Bukisa.com*, 08 Mar. 2010.
- Fisher, R.J., 'A Gift of Oranges', *America in WWII*, Dec. 2010.
- Fricke, B., '1944: Stille Nacht, unheilige Nacht, Weihnachten auf der Flucht', *Berliner Morgenpost*, 24 Dec. 2010.
- Fuhr, E., 'Wie Hitler sein letztes Weihnachtsfest verbrachte', *Welt*, 16 Dec. 2014.
- Gajek, E., 'Christmas under the Third Reich', *Anthropology today*, nr. 6, 1990.
- Groot, B. de, 'World War II: Siege of Budapest', *Historynet.com*, 06 Dec. 2006.
- Hull, M.D., 'Christmas in Embattled Bastogne', *Warfare History Network*, 01 Mai 2017.

- Kushian, J., 'Have Yourself a Nasty Little Christmas', *America in WWII*, Dec. 2010;
- Leyva, A., 'Christmas at Hanford', *Chemical Heritage Foundation*, winter 2008-2009.
- M.D., 'Christmas in Embattled Bastogne', *Warfare History Network*, 01 Mai 2017.
- Melancon, D., 'Cobra King led 4th Armored Division column that relieved Bastogne during Battle of the Bulge', *Army Europe Public Affairs Office*, 25 Feb. 2009.
- Németh, M., 'During and after the Siege of Budapest (1944-1945), *Hungarian Review*, 14 Jan. 2015.
- O'Neill, J.H., 'The True Story of the Patton Prayer', *The New American*, 12 Jan. 2004.
- Ohira, R., 'Fritz Vincken, bakery owner, dead at 69', *Honolulu Advertiser*, 11 Jan. 2002.
- Perry, J., 'Nazifying Christmas: Political Culture and Popular Celebration in the Third Reich', *Central European History*, Dec. 2005.
- Prior, J.T., 'The Night Before Christmas – Bastogne, 1944', *The Onondaga County Medical Society Bulletin*, December 1972.
- Risbey, P.N., 'Air Raid Precautions - Deaths and injuries 1939-45', 2002.
- Roberts, S., 'Augusta Chiwy, 'Forgotten' Wartime Nurse, Dies at 94', *The New York Times*, 25 Aug. 2015.
- Sassaman, R., 'Hope to the front', *Stars in WWII / America in WWII*, 2010.
- Saxon, W., 'President Cites a Story of Peace amid the Terrors of Battle', *The New York Times*, 06 Mai 1985.
- Toomey, E., 'The Manhattan Project at Hanford Site', *Atomic Heritage Foundation*, 01 Mar. 2016.
- Upadhyay, D., 'How a 'theatre play' evoked Stalin to revive Christmas tree tradition in Russia', *Russia & India Report*, 02 Jan. 2013.
- Vincken, F. 'Truce in the Forest', *Reader's Digest*, Jan. 1973, 111-114.
- Zebrowski, C., 'That Chestnut Song', *America in WWII*, Dec. 2010.

WEBSITES:

- 225th AAA Searchlight Battalion Veterans Association: Skylighters.org
- Bastogne Barracks: www.bastogne-barracks.be
- BBC WW2 People's War: www.bbc.co.uk/history/ww2peopleswar
- Bigonville in World War II: www.bigonville.info
- Canadian War Museum: www.warmuseum.ca
- Chicago Tribune Archive: chicagotribune.newspapers.com
- Database of Righteous Among The Nations: db.yadvashem.org/righteous
- Delpher / Koninklijke Bibliotheek: www.delpher.nl
- Digitale bibliotheek voor de Nederlandse letteren: www.dbnl.org
- Elliot Clan Society: www.elliotclan.com
- FDR Presidential Library: fdrlibrary.org
- Feldgrau.com: www.feldgrau.com
- German Propaganda Archive Calvin College: research.calvin.edu/german-propaganda-archive
- Historical Hotels Then & Now: www.historichotelsthenandnow.com/trianonpalaceversailles
- History.com, www.history.com
- Hong Kong Veterans Commemorative Association: www.hkvca.ca
- Huygens ING digitaal archief: resources.huygens.knaw.nl
- Ibiblio / The Public's Library and Digital Archive: www.ibiblio.org
- Imperial War Museums: www.iwm.org.uk
- KZ-Gedenkstätte Neuengamme: www.kz-gedenkstaette-neuengamme.de
- Le Royal Syndicat d'Initiative de Malmedy : www.malmedy.be
- Lebendiges Museum Online: www.dhm.de/lemo
- Life Magazine via Google Books: books.google.nl/books/about/LIFE.html?id=N0EEAAAAMBAJ
- Minnesota Historical Society's Manuscripts Collection: www.mnhs.org
- Mom's Letters Home From Europe 1942 – 1945: www.crystalsw.com/pers/mom.shtml
- National Park Service: NPS.gov
- NPR Music: www.npr.org

- SHAK: www.shak1944.org
- The American Presidency Project: www.presidency.ucsb.edu
- The National WWII Museum New Orleans:
  www.nationalww2museum.org
- The Ronald Reagan Presidential Library and Museum:
  www.reaganlibrary.gov
- Tourist Info St. Vith: www.st.vith.be
- TracesofWar.com: www.tracesofwar.com
- Uboat.net: www.uboat.net
- Veterans Affairs Canada: www.veterans.gc.ca
- War History Network: warfarehistorynetwork.com
- Weblog Australians in Stalag Luft III: australiansinsliii.blogspot.nl
- WO2 Hoeksche Waard: www.wo2-hoekschewaard.nl
- World War II - Prisoners of War - Stalag Luft I:
  www.merkki.com/christmas_and_world_war_ii.htm
- WW2Today.com: ww2today.com
- Yad Vashem: www.yadvashem.org

DOCUMENTARIES:

- 'Judy Abrams: Tenuous Threads', The Azrieli Series Short Films.
- British Pathé, www.youtube.com/user/britishpathe.
- Kerst aan het front, EO Tweede Wereldoorlog documentaires, 2005.
- NOVA, 'Suzy: de mascotte van een Canadese tankbemanning', 04 Mai 2010.
- VPRO-radio Het Spoor Terug, 'Kerst 1944', 27 Dec. 1987.
- Wartime Farm Christmas Special, BBC, 2012.

ACKNOWLEDGEMENTS:

I am grateful to Jons van Dooren of the Stichting Herdenking Amerikaanse Kerstviering 1944 (Foundation for the Commemoration of the American Christmas Celebration 1944) for his help in describing the American celebration in the De Schark Cave. The Flossenbürg Concentration Camp Memorial kindly permitted me to publish the drawing by camp inmate Hugo Walleitner. Kirsten Alexander allowed me to use information about Christmas in Stalag III from her website, australiansinsliii.blogspot.com.

The publications by Joe Perry, Stanley Weintraub, Mike Brown and Matthew Litt were particularly important sources for this book. Robert Jan Noks, Gerd Van der Auwera, Fred Bolle, Wesley Dankers, Ed Woertman, Wijnand de Gelder and Auke de Vlieger of STIWOT (Foundation for Information on World War Two) contributed to this book in large measure by their corrections, feedback and other support. The cover was designed by Roger Paulissen, and Arnold Palthe took on the time consuming work of translating the text from Dutch into English. Anne Palmer took great care in editing the translation. Finally my gratitude goes to Coen Prenger for proofreading this book and all alterations and suggestions.

Printed in the USA
CPSIA information can be obtained
at www.ICGtesting.com
LVHW051557201123
764451LV00004B/218